QUILT ART
CHINESE STYLE

QUILT ART
CHINESE STYLE

**Decorate Your Home with
Creative Patchwork Designs**

By Qiao Shuang

Better Link Press

Copyright © 2019 Shanghai Press and Publishing Development Co., Ltd.

This book is edited and designed by the Editorial Committee of *Cultural China* series.

Project Design and Text: Qiao Shuang
Photograph: Zhou Feiyu
Digital Drawing: Hong Jiaxin

Translation: Jiang Yajun
Cover Design: Wang Wei
Interior Design: Li Jing, Hu Bin (Yuan Yinchang Design Studio)

Copy Editor: Susie Gordon
Editorial Assistant: Pei Zhuomin
Editors: Wu Yuezhou, Cao Yue
Editorial Director: Zhang Yicong

Senior Consultants: Sun Yong, Wu Ying, Yang Xinci
Managing Director and Publisher: Wang Youbu

ISBN: 978-1-60220-040-1

Address any comments about *Quilt Art: Chinese Style* to:

Better Link Press
99 Park Ave
New York, NY 10016
USA

or

Shanghai Press and Publishing Development Co., Ltd.
F 7 Donghu Road, Shanghai, China (200031)
Email: comments_betterlinkpress@hotmail.com

Printed in China by Shenzhen Donnelley Printing Co., Ltd.

1 3 5 7 9 10 8 6 4 2

On page 1
Fig. 1   Fabric from Moda Fabrics
I bought this blue and gray fabric years ago, and it reminds me of a typical Chinese watertown surrounded by farmlands, rivers, and lakes and shrouded in mists—an eternal theme in traditional Chinese painting.

On pages 2–3
Fig. 2   *Purity* (detail)
Height 200 cm × Width 200 cm
Artist: Zhou Liangyun
This large chenille project drew much of its inspiration from a modern architectural project. It is the result of four-month experimentation with various methods of stiching and cutting. The sharp contrasts between colors and the combination of geometric shapes give the project a sense of abstraction.

Top
Fig. 3   The *Three and All* Series (detail)
Please refer to pages 106–107.

On facing page
Fig. 4   Different fabrics with blue flower patterns.

CONTENTS

CONTENTS

Fig. 5 Different fabrics cut in blocks.

CONTENTS

Fig. 6 *Dunhuang Caissons* (Tablecloth, detail)
Height 300 cm × Width 200 cm
Artist: Qiao Shuang
The tablecloth features a caisson from the Dunhuang Grottoes in China's northwestern Gansu Province—an architectural feature typically found in the center of a richly decorated ceiling. The project feature flowers and geometric patterns highlighted against a dark blue background. The detail is one of the flower patterns.

Fig. 7 Appliqué Studio
The project features a wall in an appliqué studio, which is covered in samples of various colors, styles, and themes by appliqué lovers.

On facing page
Fig. 8 *Four Seasons*
Height 315 cm × Width 165 cm × 4 pieces
Artists: Chen Jinmin, Yuan Zhendong, and Gao Manman
This joint project shows what is seen in different seasons through a window in a traditional building in a Suzhou Guarden. The combinations of heavy, stifling colors are impressionistic, while the window edges are abstract and deconstructive, successfully integrating Western artistic features into traditional Chinese art forms.

Preface

It must have been a million-to-one chance that I was introduced to the craft of patchwork and fell in love with it. A year later, as a lecturer at Nanjing University of the Arts, I offered to teach it and work with my students on our own projects. While my experience with the craft over the past ten years is far from enough to make me a "seasoned" patchwork artist, it has benefited me enormously as a university lecturer, as I teach other courses in the textile design program. I am more than a little proud of the many projects that I and my students have completed.

This book showcases some of these projects. While step-by-step explanations are offered, I also focus on how the ideas were conceived, how the designs were created, and how improvements were made. In addition, as an owner of a patchwork and embroidery studio, I work with crafters from all over the country, some of whom hope to be freelance artists and some of whom simply wish to be more creative. For the past few years, I have helped many of them reach satisfaction with their projects. Some of cases are analyzed in this book, which I believe will be a source of inspiration for readers.

Fig. 9 *A Kingfisher*
Height 30 cm × Width 30 cm
Artist: Qiao Shuang
The project is the result of an extensive modification of an original design due to the bird in the background. The slanting bamboo branches and the bird form make up a typical composition in Chinese painting. The colors and the patterns of the fabric are always a source of inspiration.

CHAPTER 1
Patchwork: A Brief History

Patchwork is often defined as a form of needlework that involves sewing pieces of fabric together into a larger design. Sometimes, pieced quilts are also known as patchworks. In the latter case, the larger piece becomes the top of a three-layered quilt, with the middle as the batting and the bottom as the backing.

Fig. 10 A Quilt
Height 150 cm × Width 150 cm
Artist: Qiao Shuang
All the pieces in this project were created individually during my appliqué course learning, but together they form a great traditional geometric quilt cover.

It is virtually impossible to trace the origins of patchwork as a craft (fig. 10), because natural fabric does not often stand the test of time. It is generally believed that the earliest example of patchwork is the wrapper around the body of an Egyptian Pharaoh, which is believed to date back as far as 5,000 years. The Mongolians are also believed to have been appliqué masters as early as 100 BC–AD 200.

The surviving examples of patchwork robes used by Buddhist monks and priests in the Tang dynasty (618–907) show that the Chinese employed advanced sewing techniques. Remains of pieced silk fabric from the 6th to the 9th century were also found in the cave where the Buddha Shakyamuni is believed to have lived. As the cave is located along the ancient Silk Road connecting China to Western Europe, archeologists generally agree that it must have come from China.

The oldest surviving example of patchwork in Europe features human figures and decorative motifs, and was used by the wealthy in wedding ceremonies in the 14th century.

Patchwork originated in early times, probably to keep out the cold or recycle worn clothing, but it gradually served an aesthetic purpose. In Europe, for example, evidence has been found that patterned cotton cloth from India, which was more expensive than wool, was used as a material for patchwork. As a general household could not afford washable cloth with exotic motifs, patchwork must have been a hobby only for the nobility and the wealthy.

The European tradition of patchwork was taken to the New World by the Pilgrims, where an American variety was developed using local materials. Ignoring the decorative elements of the European fashion, this variety featured simple patterns and depictions of local life and culture. Patchwork has enjoyed a widespread revival in the United States, and is now an art form that attracts designers, producers, researchers, and collectors.

The techniques for patchwork in different parts of the world share strong similarities, although some enjoy a much longer history. As the craft evolves, with up-to-date technologies and information shared across cultures and borders, patchwork lovers around the world have a much better understanding of it, cementing it as a valuable art form (fig. 11).

Fig. 11 *Leaf Scrolls* (Clutchbag)
Artist: Qiao Shuang
This artist likes to use a whole piece fabric for her clutchbags, taking maximum advantage of the material itself. The fabric for this bag has dark blue as its dominant color, but the leaf scroll with golden edges is a Chinese traditional pattern. Leaf scrolls can be a successive S-shape arrangement of various forms of the lotus, the orchid, or the peony.

Fig. 12 *Life* (detail)
Height 200 cm × Width 70 cm × 3 pieces
Artist: Yin Yue
Benefitting from a combination of oil painting and traditional Chinese painting techniques, this project depicts the changeability of life through contrasting colors.

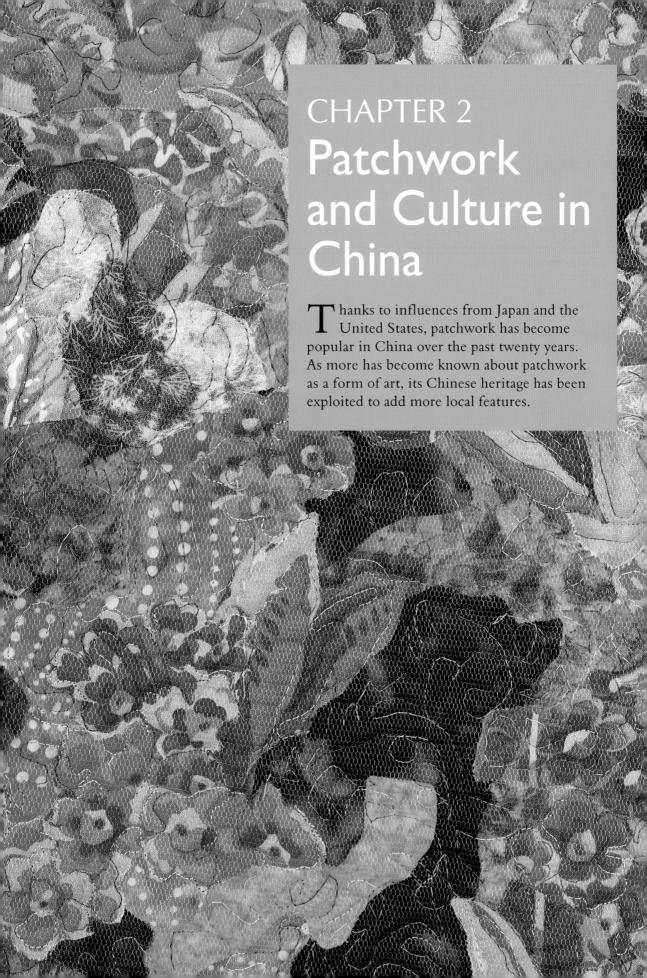

CHAPTER 2
Patchwork and Culture in China

Thanks to influences from Japan and the United States, patchwork has become popular in China over the past twenty years. As more has become known about patchwork as a form of art, its Chinese heritage has been exploited to add more local features.

Fig. 13 Imperial Theatrical Coat for Court Lady

Qing Dynasty

Metropolitan Museum of Art, New York

This jacket with skirt was made for a theatrical ensemble in Qing court. Exquisite theatrical costumes for troupes were greatly valued and passed down from generation to generation. In this patchwork, small patches are used for sleeves and hems, and the shoulders are appliquéd.

1. Patchwork Techniques: *Baina* and *Duixiu*

Traditionally, patchwork is known in China as *baina* or *duixiu*, depending on whether smaller pieces are stitched or appliquéd together. The batting can be additional (fig. 13).

A *baina* robe is made from many pieces (hence, *bai*, "a hundred") stitched (hence, *na*, "stitch") together. Known as *kasaya*, it was originally used by Buddhist monks, who made their own robes from discarded clothes as a practice of monastic discipline against worldly possessions. The mention of *baina* in a poem by Su Shi (1037–1101) from the Song dynasty (960–1279) indicates that patchwork has a history of at least 1,000 years in China.

The silk patchwork in the British Museum—probably a *kasaya*—is believed to have been made by piecing together blocks with various patterns and embroidered flowers. It shows advanced technologies with decorative features (fig. 14).

The skill of *baina* was also popular in China for children's dresses. Known as *baijia yi*, these traditional clothes were made with cloth pieces from different families in a village. These garments were believed to carry blessings from the neighbors to help children grow and

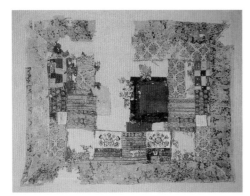

Fig. 14 Large Rectangular Patchwork

Tang dynasty

Height 51 cm × Width 49 cm

British Museum

This *baina* piece was made by embroidering small patches of fabrics of silk and twill damask. It is obviously owned by a wealthy household.

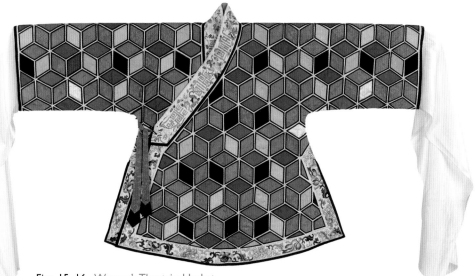

Figs. 15–16 Woman's Theatrical Jacket
Qing dynasty
85.1 cm × 289.6 cm
Metropolitan Museum of Art, New York

This long-sleeved theatrical costume was made for a female role in Chinese opera. Moving the long sleeves to express dramatic meanings is one's of the skills that performers need to master. They are called "water sleeves," as their movements resemble ripples spreading across a pool. Here, diamond patches of various colors from the background, while with the thin black edge of the hem and the embroidered floral patterns on it show the quality of both the materials and the workmanship.

protect them from diseases and other calamities. The clothes were often designed according to the colors, patterns, and shapes of the materials, and were sewn with great care and remarkable skill.

Baina was used for adults' clothes as well. A typical woman's dress in the Ming dynasty (1368–1644) would have been made by piecing small sheets of cloth in square and diamond shapes. As such, it was known as a "paddy field dress" (figs. 15–16). It is reported that in the last years of the dynasty, when extravagant lifestyles became the fashion of the day, gentlewomen's paddy field dresses would

Fig. 17 *Quilt Cover*

Collector: Wang Zengye

This quilt cover from Hechi—an ethic Zhuang area in Guangxi Province that is well known for its appliqué crafts—was made in the first half of 20th century. The delicate flowers and rich colors give it a strong ethnic flavor.

have been made using whole bolts of expensive silk.

China enjoys a long history of appliqué, which is closely related to patchwork. Appliqué can be traced back to the Northern and Southern dynasties (420–589), when similar sewing skills were practiced in Hubei Province in the middle reaches of the Yangtze River. In the culturally and economically developed Tang dynasty, it became an art of its own: *duixiu* ("multi-layer embroidery")—a complicated process of cutting, appliquéing, and sewing different fabrics. One surviving example is the well-known appliqué *thangka*—a Tibetan Buddhist art form. The complex

Fig. 18 *Tibeten Thanka of Buddha Ushnisha Vijaya*

Qing dynasty
Height 61.2 cm × Width 45 cm
Palace Museum, Beijing

This thanka depicts Ushnisha Vijaya (Namgyalma)—a powerful Buddha of longevity and auspiciousness—who has three faces, eight arms, and a crown over her long curly hair. A typical *duixiu*, it features satin patches of red, pink, yellow, apricot, blackish green, dark blue, light blue, bluish white, and light green, embroidered on a blue damask background. The techniques are similar to those that are commonly employed today, and the colors are elegent and harmonious. This item shows the quality of appliqué techniques in ancient China.

process of producing the scroll-banner painting starts with a detailed drawing on a cotton canvas. Fabrics of various colors and natures are then cut out for different areas and sewn together. Embroidery is used only to highlight some details. The raised center of an appliqué *thangka* gives it a strong three-dimensional effect, which is clear in a silk scroll depicting Usnisavijaya from the 18th century, in the collection of the Palace Museum in Beijing (fig. 18).

Duixiu is also found in household products, which often have an added layer of batting between the woven cloth top and back, to highlight their dimensions and layering. Featuring contrasts between colors and unadorned patterns, they produce an unparalleled visual effect (fig. 17).

2. Patchwork Culture

As a trained artist myself, I began by creating patchwork projects using more abstract, Westernized images (fig. 19). However, I soon began to experiment with traditional Chinese symbols and images, showing my own understanding of my heritage as well as conceptualizations of modern art.

Chinese Painting

During my formal education I was taught how to design in the Western artistic tradition, yet Chinese painting and aesthetics have always been an important part of my professional career.

Traditional painting is done with a brush dipped in water, black ink, or colored pigments. The most popular materials for paintings are silk or paper, and the finished works are mounted on scrolls. They are classified into three subject categories: figure paintings, bird-and-flower paintings, and landscape paintings. The two main techniques are *gongbi*, meaning "meticulous," and ink and wash painting. The former uses highly detailed brushstrokes that delimit exact details, and is often highly colored; the latter features sketchy brushstrokes in a freehand style, allowing an artist to express their emotions.

For centuries, Chinese painting has been considered as a highly complicated form

Fig. 19 *50-Meter Deep Blue*
Height 200 cm × Width 200 cm
Artist: Qiao Shuang
This work expresses the artist's early understandings of abstraction and deconstructivism, representing colorful underwater sunlight.

Fig. 20 *Finches and Bamboo*
Zhao Ji (Emperor Huizong of the Song Dynasty, 1082–1135)
Ink and color on silk
Height 33.8 cm × Width 55.5 cm
Metropolitan Museum of Art, New York

This painting, featuring two finches on branches jutting from a cliff, exemplifies the realistic style of flower-and-bird painting practiced at the emperor's academy. The composition and coloring techniques can be well employed in appliquéing to create a similar sense of artistic beauty.

of visual art, second only to calligraphy. It depicts subjects from daily life, and also displays emotions, poetic meanings, and philosophical conceptualizations. The well-known "literati paintings" were mostly the work of painters who had traveled extensively, expressing their understandings of nature and the world more widely. These artistic elements would definitely lend your patchwork projects a uniquely Chinese aesthetic touch (figs. 20–21).

Fig. 21 Wall Hanging of the *Three and All* Series (detail)
This part of the project was undertaken in the Song style of the bird-and-flower painting. Note how the subtle changes in colors for the leaves and bamboo add to the unity of design and the hierarchical relationship of the elements (see pages 106–107).

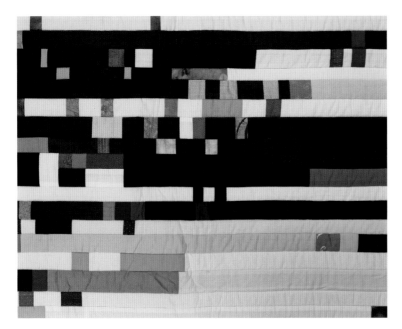

Fig. 22 *Garden on a Snowy Day*
Height 200 cm × Width 200 cm
Artist: Qiao Shuang
This work shows a garden in Suzhong on a snowy day in late winter, highlighting the famous black and white straight-edged walls. While bare branches dominate the design, budding leaves are growing against the ice and snow.

Gardening

China has a gardening history of more than three thousand years. As a distinctive presence in traditional Chinese architecture, its ultimate purpose is freedom. The best garden is believed to be one "constructed by man but as if done by nature." Legend had it that Qin Shi Huang (259–210 BC), the first emperor of a unified China, had a Daoist Shanglin Garden built, featuring high mountains and impenetrable forests, rivers and waterfalls, streams and lakes, and flowers and animals. No one knows where the garden was, but the *Ode to Shanglin Garden* by Sima Xiangru (c. 179–118 BC), a writer in the Western Han dynasty (202 BC–8), tells us that it was the best part of the emperor's land, rather than one made by his subjects. This aligns with the dominant Daoist Theory of Lao Zi (571–471 BC) and Zhuang Zi (369–286 BC), who defined *dao* as the origin of the universe and everything in it. They promoted the philosophical conceptualizations that "man is part of nature" and that "nature is quietly beautiful." This heritage was preserved in the Ming and Qing dynasties, when "literati gardens" were constructed to imitate natural landscapes in places that were much smaller than royal gardens, such as the Summer Palace.

Elements in gardening—gray tiles, white walls, wooden windows, and seasonal scenery—can be exploited to add a Chinese touch to projects (figs. 22–23).

Fig. 23 Perforated Windows in Suzhou Gardens
This style of ornamental window has perforation inlaid in the walls or doors. It provides an opening for ventilation and lighting, but also acts as a picture frame through which to capture the vistas beyond. As such, it can be a great source of inspiration in appliquéing.

Fig. 24 *Buddhist Sessions: Lotus Flower*
Height 540 cm × Width 1000 cm
Artist: Qiao Shuang

Now part of the collection at Nanjing's Dabao'en Temple, this creative work featuring 202 figures of the Buddha involves about 45,000 pieces of various fabric. It also required exhaustive research into references and paintings of Buddhist figures.

Among the many symbolic patterns and propitious marks in Buddhist art and literature, the lotus flower blooms profusely, often in the hand of a beautiful female Bodhisattva in statue form. Chinese people believe that the lotus has its roots in muddy water, but the flower rises above the mud to bloom clean and fragrant. The lotus flower has been a symbol of purity, a metaphor for a person who refuses to flow with the tide of insanity.

Culturally Significant Patterns

Symbolism in Chinese culture reflects how its people as a group define "beauty." Implied meanings, such as luck, are often represented by means of homonyms and symbolism.

Characters or words in Chinese that have different forms can be homonyms, of which the concrete is often used to represent the abstract. A good example is images of a bat, which are often seen on household items because the second syllable of *bianfu* ("bat") is a homonym of the character for "happiness" (*fu*). Symbolism is another means by which abstract ideas, concepts, or emotions are shown by objects around us. For example, the four plants known as the "Four Gentlemen" —the plum blossom, the orchid, the bamboo, and the chrysanthemum—are traditionally compared to four

attributes of a Confucianist *junzi*, or "gentleman." Cloud vector patterns, which represent progress and auspiciousness, are often seen on chinaware, embroidery work, or jade items.

Think about adding some of these images to your own creations, in addition to changes in the background and color combinations (fig. 24).

Both traditional painting and gardening highlight the link between an object and what it means. The object is no more than a reference by which an artist engages in expression. Chinese art occupies a turning point from reason to feeling and from what is seen to what is felt, and artists are turning to themselves for inspiration. This is why I have turned to my own heritage for a means of expressing myself with my projects.

Fig. 25 The *Three and All* Series (detail)
Please refer to pages 106–107.

CHAPTER 3
Before You Start

This chapter explains what you need as a patchwork beginner (tools, supplies, and fabric), and how to choose them for your own projects.

1. Fabric

Patchwork involves pieces of fabric of various colors and patterns, which are given a new lease of life through cutting and matching.

Fibers

For most patchwork beginners, 100% plain-woven fabric is the number one choice. It is easier to work with for a variety of designs, either by hand or by machine, if medium thickness and sturdiness are chosen.

Heavyweight fabrics like denim, linen, and canvas are heavier and thicker than your basic cotton calico, and as such are better for machine use.

The slippery and smooth texture of silk poses some difficulties, and requires special care when making marks, cutting, and sewing. It is often a favorite of more advanced crafters, who are more skilled in exploiting other functional materials as background fabric. As it originates from the cocoons of silkworms, it is easily manipulated by using acid dyes to create attractive colors. Some patchwork artists prefer hand-dyed silk.

Types of Fabric

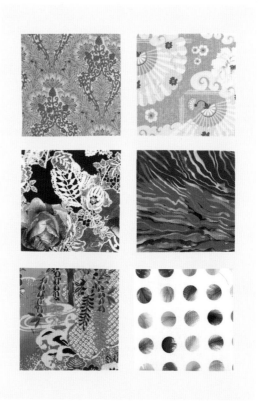

Plain fabric is fabric of a single color. There is no clear distinction between the right and wrong sides. Plain fabric from different manufacturers may differ in terms of richness and warmth of color, which might be preferable to some artists but not to others.

The most popular hand-dyed fabric among patchwork artists is probably the type that comes from Bali, Indonesia, due to its smoother, thinner, but stiffer texture and its unique watercolors. Other hand-dyeing techniques feature distinctive visual effects from the Batik method. Hand-dyed fabric is often used to produce a watercolor or water-and-ink touch.

Printed fabric has a definite right side in contrast with the wrong side, as it is the result of applying colors to plain fabric in definite patterns or designs by methods such as screen printing or cylinder printing. Digital textile printing, a process of printing on textiles using specialized inkjet technology, is now becoming popular, and has led to the availability of fabric with more complicated patterns and more color combinations.

Yarn-dyed fabric, which is especially popular among patchwork lovers in Asia, gets its distinctive appearance and feel from how it is woven: the thread (or yarn) has been dyed before weaving. It is often tougher, and is therefore suitable for projects such as bags and cushions.

2. Tools and Supplies

Various tools are needed during different stages of creating a patchwork, from designing to sewing. They include:

Needles

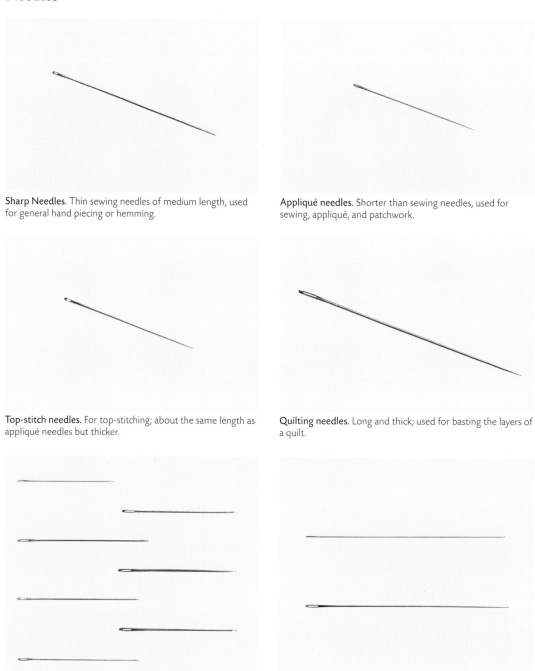

Sharp Needles. Thin sewing needles of medium length, used for general hand piecing or hemming.

Appliqué needles. Shorter than sewing needles, used for sewing, appliqué, and patchwork.

Top-stitch needles. For top-stitching; about the same length as appliqué needles but thicker.

Quilting needles. Long and thick; used for basting the layers of a quilt.

Embroidery needles. Various lengths, eye sizes, and thickness; used in embroidery, and available for different threads or strands.

Beading needles. Long, thin needles with a very narrow eye to slip easily through sequins or beads.

Finger Protectors

A **thimble** is traditionally worn on the index finger of your sewing hand to add friction, making it easier for you to pull a needle out of a thick layer of fabric. It is especially useful in basting, top-stitching, or fastening a purse frame onto your clutch.

A **metal ring thimble** is traditionally worn on the middle finger like a ring, allowing you to push or pull a needle through your work.

A **leather ring thimble** works like a metal one, but provides a better fit and greater comfort when you are working with heavier fabric.

Accessories

A **pincushion** is a small, thick pad made of cloth, used to hold needles when they are not being used.

A **sewing magnet** is great for picking up straight pins with ease and keeping them in a safe place until required.

A **needle threader** has a thin and flexible wire at one end, which helps to put thread through the eye of a needle. At the other end is a thread cutter, which is a perfect replacement for scissors to cut threads. This device is great when you are working with multiple threads in embroidery, and is convenient to carry when you travel.

Safety pins are used to hold the top, batting, and backing in place. It is sometimes a better choice than basting.

Appliqué pins. Shorter than straight pins; used in hand appliquéing to temporarily hold pieces of fabric together.

Straight pins (pearlized head). Pins with sharp points, about the length of a sharp needle; useful in piecing by hand for temporarily fastening pieces of fabric together. They may be ironed over safely.

Straight pins (flower head). Pins with a flat head, which are convenient when working with a sewing machine. A wide range of sizes is available for various types of fabric.

A **seam ripper** is a sharp pointed tool that you use to rip out a seam when you make a mistake. It is perfect replacement for scissors, for effortless and accurate seam ripping.

A **roller** is a tool used for pressing seams. It is superior to the iron in piecing smaller blocks, and is great for travel.

A **bias tape maker** is used to make bias tapes, and is especially useful in making wall-hangings or creating smaller projects. A wide variety of bias tape maker options are available, and the 18 mm version is used for the projects in this book.

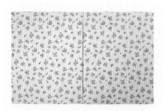 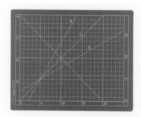 

An **ironing board** provides an ideal surface for removing wrinkles from fabric, ironing batting onto fabric, or pressing a completed project flat for a better finish. A high-quality ironing board is sturdy and firm.

A **cutting mat** is a self-healing rubber mat that is used to protect surfaces when cutting fabric with a rotary cutter. The measurements printed on it allow you to cut accurately.

An **iron** is used to press the fabric before it is sewn, or to flatten a project in order to finish it.

 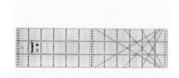 

The metal **frame fastener** is designed to hold a metal clutch frame in place before you sew it onto your bag.

A **patchwork ruler** with scales and lines is a great help for drawing and measuring.

The **grid paper** used in patchwork is usually opaque or semi-transparent regular graphing paper. The most common type has a calibration of 0.5 cm grids.

Used in textile and art projects, **tracing paper** is thin and transparent.

Embroidery hoops or frames come in different shapes and sizes. The one used for the projects in this book was a rectangle frame that can be attached to a tabletop.

Marking Tools

A **mechanical fabric pencil** is designed to make temporary markings on cloth or to draw on paper pattern. It is soft, and comes in a variety of colors.

An **erasable water pen** is a marking tool for fabric. The ink usually lasts longer than an erasable air pen, and can be removed instantly with a dab of water. It is often used to mark the right side of fabric, or for long-term projects.

An **erasable air pen** is used for marking the right side of fabric. The ink evaporates in 24 to 48 hours. It is used to make temporary markings, or for short-term projects.

Cutting Tools

Crafting scissors are used to cut paper patterns, plastic boards, or thin wires. All-purpose scissors work well.

Dressmaker's shears have long blades and blunt tips, and are used only to cut fabric. Using them for other purposes may harm the blades.

Embroidery scissors are designed to cut smaller pieces of fabric, or to form them into specific shapes. They are often used for appliqué stitch.

Pinking scissors have Z-shaped blades and are designed for making small cuts. Embroidery scissors can serve the same purpose, and are an ideal replacement.

A **thread clipper** is a small, short-bladed tool used for snipping threads in machine sewing. You don't need one if your machine has a built-in thread cutter.

A **rotary cutter** is a circular blade with a handle, and can easily cut multiple layers of clothing.

Sewing Threads

Hand-sewing thread is used in piecing by hand. It is usually white, but other colors are sometimes preferred, to match the color of the fabric for appliquéing.

Top-stitching threads are heavier than hand-sewing threads. They are often used in hand sewing to top-stitch and match the fabric in color.

Basting threads are for long-running stitches temporarily created by hand or machine to hold fabric in place before the final stitching. Basting stitches are easily removed by hand.

Bobbin threads are the threads that are inserted into a sewing machine. Some types are machine only, but others are not. To differentiate, refer to the instructions on the package.

Machine embroidery threads come in many colors. Different from ordinary bobbin threads, they are often silky, and are used in the machine sewing of appliquéd pieces on top of a project, top-stitching, or stitching for decorative purposes. They are used in the embroidered beading project in the tutorial in this book.

Threads for embroidery are available in a wide range of fibers including cotton, silk, metallic, or synthetic. The one used in the tutorial is size 25 cotton.

Lining and Backing

There are two types of **batting**, for a sewing machine and for hand sewing. Some are fusible and other are not. The fusible side is not as smooth as the opposite side. They are made of different materials and are available in different weights.

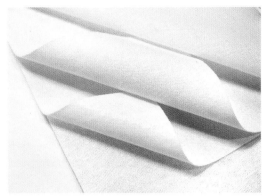

Adhesive interlining is used beneath a fabric to provide stability and support. A wide range is available in terms of roughness and thickness. It can be adhesive on one side or both sides.

A **fusible tear-away stabilizer** is a double-sided iron-on adhesive used for appliqué. The right side is smoother than the wrong side.

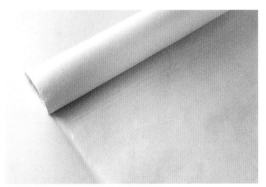

Freezer paper is very handy to have in your sewing room. You can trace the outline of your pattern onto the dull side, just as you do on regular paper. You can also iron the waxy side to stick it to fabric temporarily, and then tear it off easily. Freezer paper is often used as paper pattern in appliquéing.

Embellishments

Beads of various shapes, sizes, and colors bring dimension to fabric in embroidery. High-quality glass beads are easy to work with using proper needles, and can serve as sparkly decorative objects.

Like beads, **spangles**, **sequins**, or **paillettes** are decorative pieces. They are usually made from metal or plastic, and have a hole through which they can be sewn to a project. They are made in different colors, sizes, and shapes. Their qualities are often judged in terms of color, coating, and position of the hole.

Fig. 26 *Life* (detail)
Please refer to page 15.

CHAPTER 4
Basic
Techniques

The projects in the following chapters are mostly machine-made, but some are made by hand. This chapter introduces the basic techniques for the two categories, for a target readership of beginners.

1. Terms

The terms used in the book are as follows:

Seam allowance: The area between the stitching and the raw, cut edge of the fabric.

Net measurement: Measurements on drawing sketches or on finished products.

Cutting measurement: Measurements including seam allowance, sometimes used in drawing sketches.

Paper pattern: A template of sturdy materials like paperboard from which the parts of a design are traced onto fabric before being cut out.

Stitching line: Actual lines of various types that are traced onto the fabric on which you sew, indicating where the seam should be made.

Seam direction: The side or sides to which seams are pressed and ironed. Seams usually face the side of fabric that have darker colors or dominant patterns, but sometimes two sides are preferred.

- All measurements in this book are in centimeters.
- Measurements of final pieces are net measurements unless indicated and marked on dimensional drawings. A seam allowance of 1 cm needs to be maintained for a small square in hand stitching, and 0.7 cm trimmed when finished; a seam allowance of 0.7 cm is needed in machine stitching; the seam allowance for appliqué varies from one design to another.
- Quilting projects usually become smaller in size, and the difference varies depending on fabric type, thickness of battings, stitch density, and stitching technique.
- Thread of a similar color to the fabric is suggested for appliquéing and top-stitching. To highlight the stitches for the reader, thread of contrasting colors is used in the illustrations.

Fig. 27 *The Starry Sky*
Height 200 cm × Width 200 cm
Artist: Zhao Yan

With carefully chosen pink and blue patches, this project features a starry sky seen through a kaleidoscope. It benefits from a technique called "shadow appliqué" which involves placing a transparent or semi-transparent screen over the covering fabric before top-stitching.

2. Running Stitches

The samples in the book are mostly machine work, but hand stitching was involved for some of them. The basic techniques for hand and machine stitching are as follows.

Hand Sewing: Blocks

As a craft with a long history, patchwork projects that use traditional hand stitching are valued more highly. In addition, human crafters are able to do things that machines are not. Even for beginners, learning to stitch can be simple.

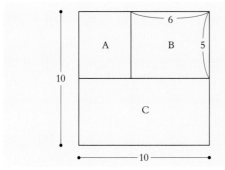

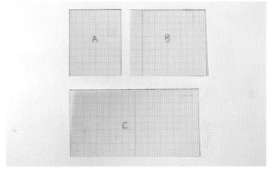

1 Draw the patterns on paper as designed, and identify them as A, B, and C. Cut the paper for the patterns. When a same pattern is repeated in the design, only one pattern is required.

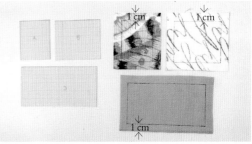

2 Place a pattern on the wrong side of a patch of well-pressed fabric, and outline it on the fabric with a pen. Make sure that the corners are clearly marked for pins, which will later be used to hold the fabric in place.

3 Allow a seam allowance of 1 cm all round, for all the patches.

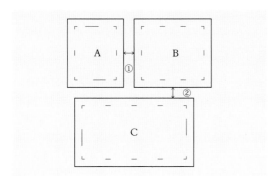

4 Decide on the order to join the patches.

5 Place the first two patches (A and B) together, with the right sides together and the stitching lines aligned.

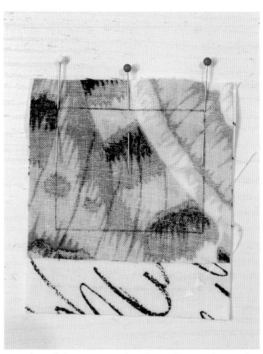

6 Place a straight pin at each end of a line and then another in the middle, making sure they are right out from the line on the wrong side. Another straight pin can be used between the neighboring two when needed. A distance of about 2 cm is suggested for beginners.

7 When all the pins are in place, fasten them. Make sure that the stitching lines are in place.

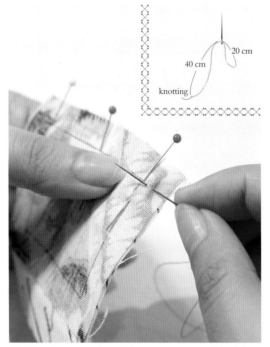

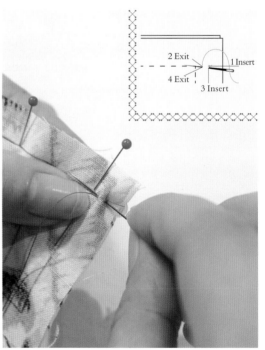

8 Thread your needle until the segment on one side of the eye is about twice as long as the other. Tie a knot at the end of the longer one. Insert the needle into the fabric about 0.5 cm away from where two stitching lines meet, and exit around the middle toward the corner.

9 Repeat what you have done in the same place, resulting in a so-called "back-stitch." This is required in hand stitching at the beginning or end of stitching, to keep the stitches from being pulled out.

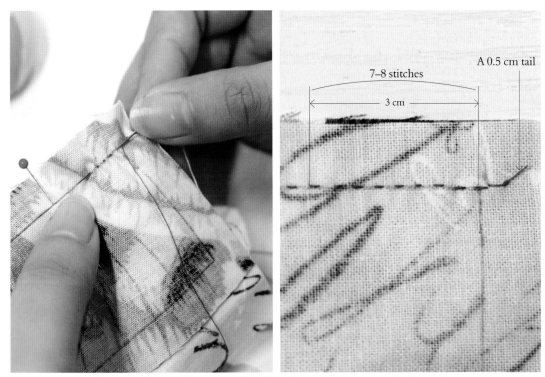

7–8 stitches

3 cm

A 0.5 cm tail

10 Insert the needle into the fabric at the starting point, and continue to work along the stitching line. You may exit every 3–4 stitches. An average length of 7–8 stitches for 3 cm is suggested. The straight pins need to be removed when you approach them. Fabric can be easily distorted if you pull the thread too tightly; if this happens, you can use your fingernail to smooth it back.

A seam allowance of about 0.7 cm

11 Insert or exit through the pin hole at the end, which gives a professional finished appearance. Continue your work for 0.5 cm before back-stitching. Tie an overhand knot with the end, leaving a 0.5 cm tail.

12 Snip the edge, leaving a seam allowance of about 0.7 cm.

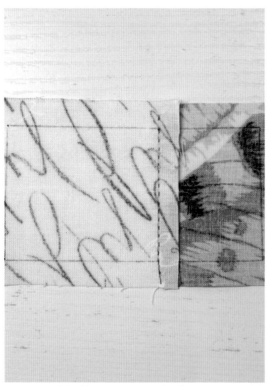

13 Spread the fabric out and press the allowance to the side of patch A. Press the seam open using the tip of your fingernail or a seam stick before you iron it.

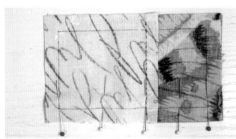

14 Join your finished work with patch C (right sides together), as you did with patches A and B. Hold them together securely with pins.

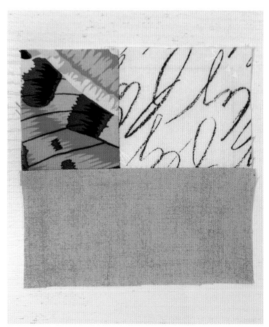

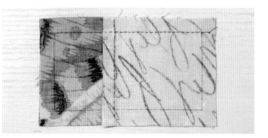

15 Again, start from about 0.5 cm away from where the stitching lines meet. Continue your work with a length of 7–8 stitches very 3 cm, and finish at the point 0.5 cm away from the end of the stitching line. Remember to back-stitch at the beginning and at the end of stitching. The added layers of seam allowance may prevent you from exiting every 3–4 stitches when you meet them, and you may exit every stitch.

16 Trim the edge of the allowance. Spread the whole patch open and run an iron over the seam. Sit back and enjoy!

Machine Sewing: Blocks of the Same Size

Compared with hand sewing, machine sewing has its advantages: a machine is faster than your hands; you don't need paper patterns, sewing lines, or straight pins; and you use a rotary cutter for layers of fabric. Most importantly, it saves you time! That's why I've used my machine for most of the projects in the tutorial. In this section, I explain the basic skills for sewing small square blocks.

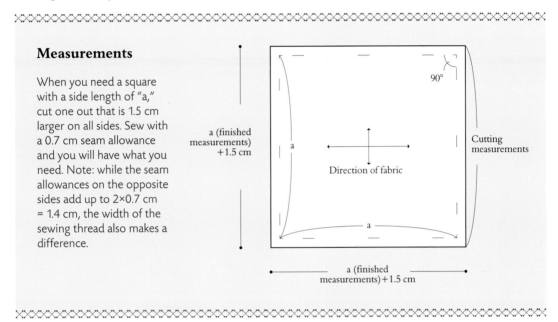

Measurements

When you need a square with a side length of "a," cut one out that is 1.5 cm larger on all sides. Sew with a 0.7 cm seam allowance and you will have what you need. Note: while the seam allowances on the opposite sides add up to 2×0.7 cm = 1.4 cm, the width of the sewing thread also makes a difference.

a (finished measurements) +1.5 cm

90°

a

Direction of fabric

a

Cutting measurements

a (finished measurements) +1.5 cm

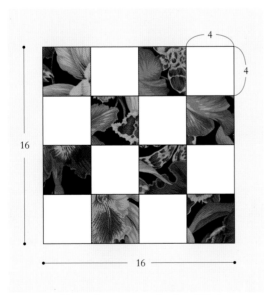

16

16

4

4

1 Cut out fabrics of contrasting colors for 16 blocks and alternate them as the illustration shows. The measurements indicated are net measurements.

2 Run your iron over your fabric on your ironing board. When working with the second piece, place it on top of the first, so that the two "stick" together, making it easier for you to use your rotary cutter, as they don't shift. The method works well for as many as 10 layers of fabric.

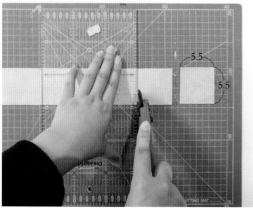

3 Transfer the two layers to your cutting mat. As your blocks have a 4 cm side length, you need to cut out eight with a side length of 5.5 cm. This means that you need two strips of 5.5 × 44 cm (5.5 × 8 cm = 44 cm). Cut them into 8 squares.

4 Alternate them on your table.

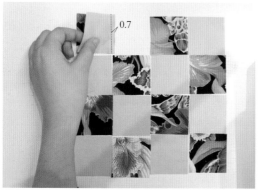

5 Lay out your two pieces of material with their right sides together and their edges aligned.

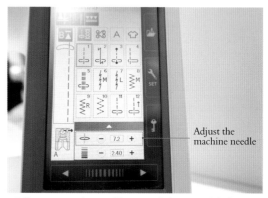

Adjust the machine needle

6 Turn your sewing machine on and choose straight line. Sew them together using chain stitching. You don't need to back-stitch. Adjust the machine needle to maintain a seam allowance of 0.7 cm. To adjust your needle accurately, you may want to refer to your guide, as machines of different brands or models may be different in this respect.

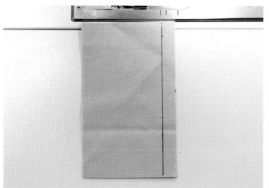

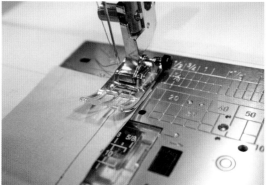

7 There are many ways to maintain a seam. My favorite techniques may be useful for beginners. As an experiment, line up two pieces and mark a 0.7 cm allowance on the top one. Place it under the presser foot, with the right edge of the fabric lining up with the right edge of the presser foot. Adjust your needle until it is directly above the sewing line. With the help of your hand wheel, check if the point of the needle is aligned with your sewing line. Remember the value for later use.

Line up the right sides of the fabric and the presser, so that you sew in a straight line, and an accurate seam allowance is obtained. If the needle position of your machine is not adjustable, you may want to mark it out on your work surface.

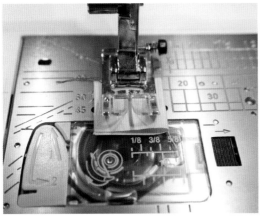

8 Find a scrap and fold it in half. Place it under the presser foot and begin to sew. This is called a "guide scrap." Note: to sew a single layer of fabric may bring about a change of tension in the thread.

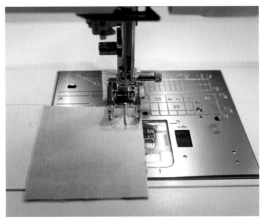

9 Place your first pair of blocks under the presser before your guide scrap comes out.

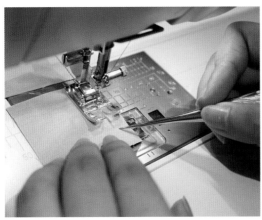

10 Sew past the pair for a while, with nothing under your presser foot. Feed in the new pair, right sides together, before the previous one is out. Do the same with the rest of the pairs.

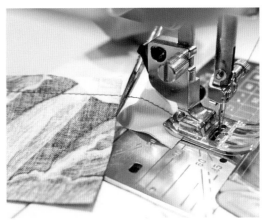

11 Find another guide scrap, fold it in half, and feed it in. When the last pair comes out, cut the connecting thread between the guide and the last pair.

12 Take the pairs away from the machine.

13 Cut all other connecting threads and arrange them as they were before being sewn.

14 Press the seam to the fabric with a darker color. Absolute beginners are suggested to open up the seam with their fingernail or a seam stick before they use their iron. The pointed tip of your iron works well. A wrinkled seam allowance results in changes in the size of the fabric.

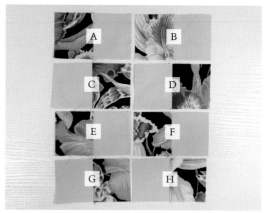

15 Number your rectangle blocks as in the picture. Place a guide scrap under the presser foot and start to sew. Feed in blocks A and B with the right sides together. Go through the remaining three pairs this way before you feed in another guide scrap. Press the seam allowances flat using the method in step 14. Lay them in place on your work table.

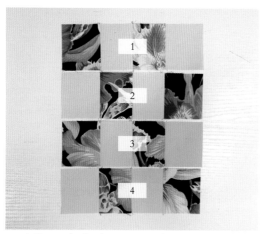

16 Line up the first larger piece with the second, with the right sides together.

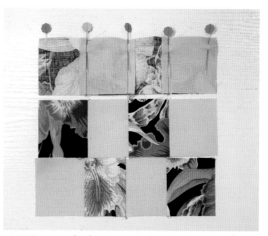

17 I suggest that beginners pin them in place. Use a flat headed straight pin at each side and along each seam. Sew them together. When you reach a pin, remove it.

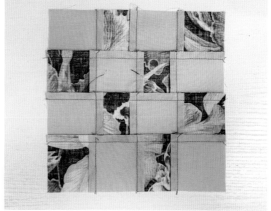

18 The seam allowance can be pressed to either side and ironed flat. Piece it with the third strip this way, and then the fourth. The direction of the seam allowances should all be the same.

Machine Sewing: Blocks of Different Sizes

These techniques are for piecing together blocks other than squares and right-angled isosceles triangles, especially shapes with straight sides.

Measurements

When you need a rectangle with side lengths of "a" and "b," cut one out that is 1.5 cm larger on all sides. Sew with a 0.7 cm seam allowance, and you will have what you need.

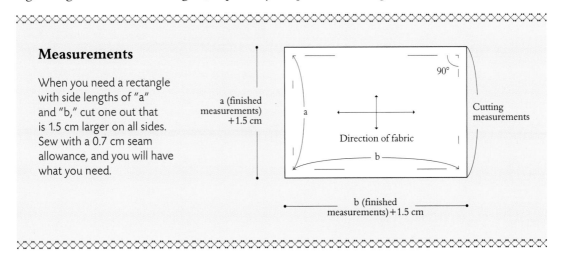

a (finished measurements) +1.5 cm

90°

Cutting measurements

Direction of fabric

b (finished measurements) +1.5 cm

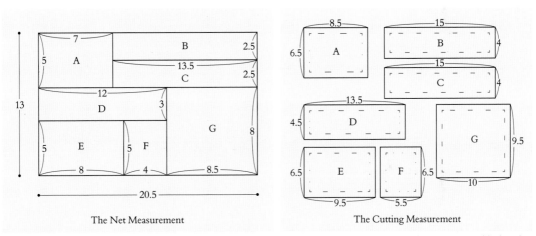

The Net Measurement

The Cutting Measurement

1 Cut out blocks of desired sizes. Remember that a seam allowance of 1.5 cm needs to be maintained. For instance, a block with net measures of 5 × 7 cm requires an unfinished material the size of (5+1.5) cm × (7+1.5) cm = 6.5 × 8.5 cm.

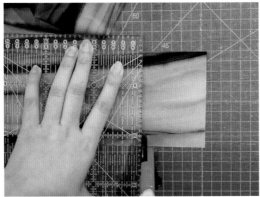

2 Press your fabric flat and cut out what you need with your rotary cutter.

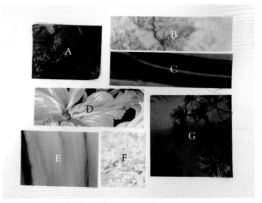

3 Place them in the order you want.

4 Number them. Piece smaller blocks together before larger ones. Work with blocks B and C first, and press the seam allowance to the side with a darker color.

5 Then piece it with block A, right sides together and edges lined up. With blocks B and C on top of block A, sew them together. Ignore the seam of blocks B and C when you reach it. Once sewn, press the seam allowance to the piece with a darker color.

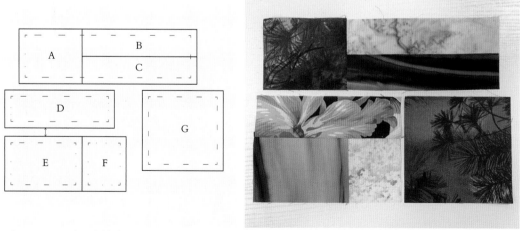

6 Continue to work with blocks E and F this way, and then piece it with block D.

7 Piece blocks D, E, and F with block G. Press all seam allowances to the side with the darker color. Where colors make no difference, choose the side that is easiest for you to iron it flat. Press the seam allowance and iron it every time you sew a new piece.

8 Sew the two larger blocks together.

9 Press the seam allowance to one side and iron it flat.

3. Machine Sewing: Appliqué

Appliquéing by machine is genuinely useful when sewing irregular shapes or curves, especially when representing animals or objects. The techniques for projects with and without a seam allowance are different. Going without a seam allowance, which is explained in this section, makes it easy for you to handle delicate details or complex patterns. However, the resulting projects are less wear-resistant and durable.

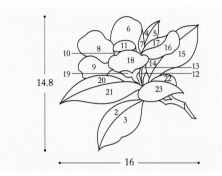

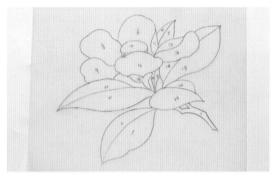

1 Transfer your flower pattern onto your tracing paper. Your lines need to be smooth, so take your time. Never repeat a line or a curve. Number all the shapes in the picture, from bottom to top.

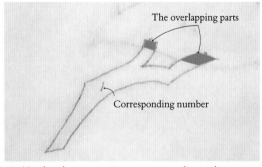

2 Turn the tracing paper over. With its right side up, place the tear-away stabilizer on top of it. Sketch all the patterns. For overlapping parts, trace them all out for a full covering of the upper patterns.

3 Number the paper patterns, corresponding to those on the tracing paper. Mark the excess so that you don't have to be extremely exact when cutting, as it will not be seen in the finished project.

4 Transfer pattern 2 onto the stabilizer, leaving a gap of 3–5 mm between the two patterns for future cutting. Again, trace it all out for the part on top of which pattern 4 will be placed.

5 Draw all the other patterns.

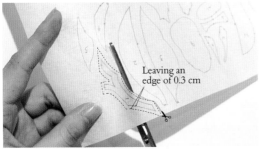

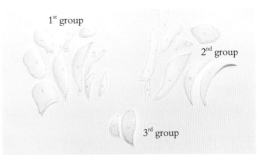

Leaving an edge of 0.3 cm

6 Cut the patterns from the stabilizer, leaving an edge of 0.2–0.3 cm.

7 Put the patterns into three groups.

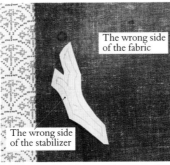

The upper edge of the tracing paper

The right side of the tracing paper

The wrong side of the stabilizer

The wrong side of the fabric

8 Cut for a background fabric of 30×30 cm. Press it well and lay it on the ironing board, with the right side facing up. Place the tracing paper on it, and hold the two in place with two straight pins on the upper edge. Iron your patches well. Lay the fabric for patch 1 on the ironing board with the wrong side facing up. Place the stabilizer on top of the fabric, with the adhesive side facing down. Run a warm iron over the stabilizer to stick it to the fabric.

9 Cut the fabric according to the stabilizer. It should be larger than the pattern. What is left can be used for other purposes. Cut the fabric and the stabilizer along the outline on the stabilizer.

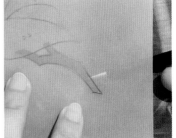

10 Remove the white film on the back of the stabilizer and you will see the adhesive substance on the fabric.

11 Lift up one end of the tracing paper. Place patch 1 on the background fabric with the right side facing up using a nipper. Re-place the tracing paper and coax the patch until it perfectly coincides with its image on the tracing paper.

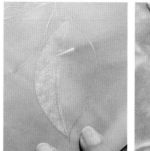

12 Check by gently lifting the tracing paper up to make sure patch 1 remains where it is. Run a warm iron (wool setting) over the right side of the fabric until it sticks to the background. Be careful that the patches don't shift. Wait until it cools down, and resume the tracing paper, which may wrinkle when hot.

13 Repeat the previous step, cut the remaining patches, and press them onto your fabric with the iron.

14 Iron all the patches onto the background fabric.

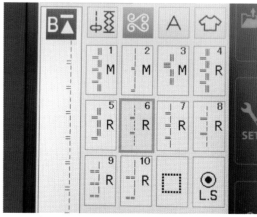

15 Choose blanket stitch on your machine, and adjust it to the appropriate stitch density and width. The default settings, which are easier to handle, are suggested for beginners.

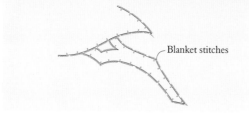

Blanket stitches

16 Choose thread that matches the fabric. The stitches show less clearly when lighter threads are used. Sew each along the edges to hold the blocks onto the right side of the fabric. Back-stitch at the beginning and the end.

17 Finish all the patches and you're done!

4. Top-Stitching

Top-stitching is a traditional sewing technique where the line of stitching is designed to be seen from the outside, either for holding the batting and the top in place or for decorative purposes. It can be done either by hand or by machine.

Top-Stitching by Hand

Batting is often used in top-stitching by hand. Before top-stitching, the three layers—the top, the batting, and the backing—need to be held securely in place with basting stitches when the batting layer is not adhesive. Wall hangings and cushions are two such examples. When adhesive batting is chosen, the top and the batting are top-stitched before the backing is added, such as when making bags. Top-stitching in this tutorial only involves adhesive batting, and the skills are explained by showing how smaller blocks are pieced together.

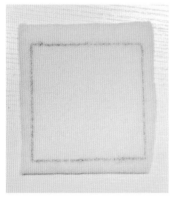

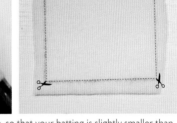

Cut along the inside of the line

1 Cut out your adhesive batting as desired. The net measurement of the top is 10 × 10 cm, so your batting should be of the same size. A pen can be used as a marker.

2 Cut it out along the inside of the line, so that your batting is slightly smaller than your top to allow the stitching lines to be seen.

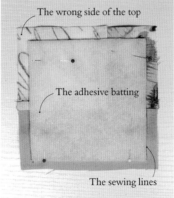

The wrong side of the top

The adhesive batting

The sewing lines

3 Trim the rough edges of your top and iron well. Lay it on your table with the wrong side facing you. Place your batting on top with the adhesive side down. Line up the edges of the batting with your sewing lines with the ink visible all around. When your batting is too large, cut it smaller using the sewing lines as reference. Hold the two layers in place with straight pins. Turn them over and lay them on your ironing board. Make sure they don't shift.

4 Set your iron to a wool setting. Carefully run it over the whole of the fabric so that the two layers stick together. Remove the pins before it is too late. Stay in one place for three seconds before moving on, so that they are securely attached to each other.

5 Check it when the top cools down.

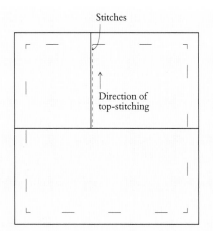

Stitches

Direction of top-stitching

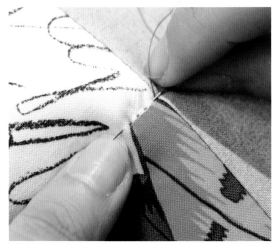

6 Top-stitch the two layers, starting from the center and working all the way down along the side without a seam allowance. You don't have to hide your stitches; neither do you need keep a distance from the sewing lines.

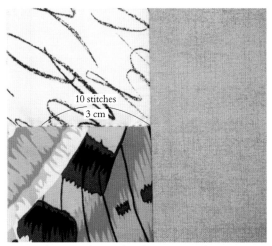

10 stitches
3 cm

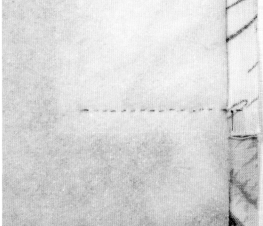

7 It is pleasing to the eye if you keep 9–10 stitches in 3 cm. You need to go beyond the outside sewing line, but no further than 5 mm.

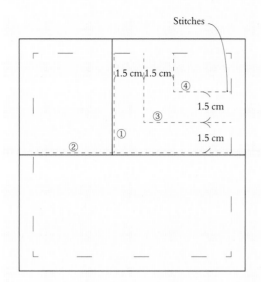

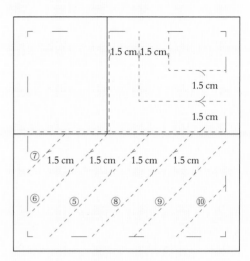

8 Finish the rest of the work. As for order, you should go from the center to the periphery.

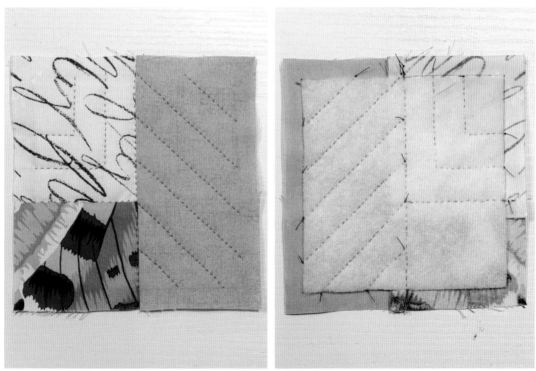

9 Large surfaces require more top-stitching work to hold the two layers more securely and to highlight the undulating surface. You can use parallel lines, diamond checks, and other geometric figures or stitches to highlight the patterns on the fabric. Top-stitching is often followed by adding backing or inside pocket fabric to your work.

Stitching in the Ditch

Machine top-stitching can be done by stitching in the ditch or in freestyle. To stitch in the ditch is to place stitches along the seam line on the side without a seam allowance or along the edges of appliquéd patterns. Free-hand stitching refers to stitching that does not take seam lines or appliquéing lines into consideration. The latter is a more advanced technique, which sewing beginners have to learn. What follows are some basics for stitching in the ditch.

Preparation before Top-Stitching by Machine

Check for any loose thread ends and trim them, as they will show easily under the top fabric. Press it with your iron. You don't have to deal with seam allowances when you are working on an appliqué project.

- When you are using a one-sided adhesive batting, press the batting to the top fabric. Top-stitch the two layers to hold them together, followed by adding backing or inside pocket fabric. This method is usually preferred when making household items such as handbags. Refer to steps in top-stitching by hand.
- When your batting is not adhesive, the top, the batting, and the backing need to be held in place before you start. Make sure that the batting is 2–5 cm larger all round than the top, and 2–5 cm smaller than the backing. Lay the well-pressed backing fabric on the table with the wrong side facing up. Place the batting in the middle, and then the top right on top of it, with the right side facing you. Hold the three layers in place at the corners with paper tape when necessary, before you use safety pins.

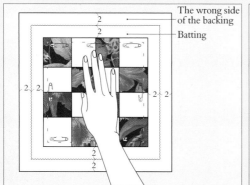 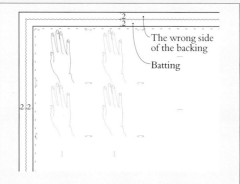

- As the project shown in the picture on the left is small, pins are spaced as indicated. The larger project on the right requires a palm-length gap between pins.

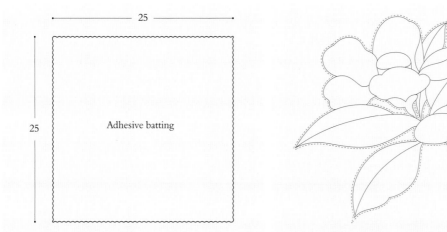

1 The following explains how to stitch in the ditch with a sewing machine for the top of an appliqué project. The pictures shows the net measurements of the batting (left) and top-stitching (right) .

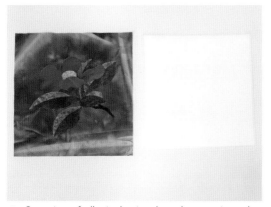

2 Cut a piece of adhesive batting about the same size as the top.

3 Iron the adhesive batting to the top.

4 Use threads that match the background in color. Start in the center, reinforce the backstitch several times to secure your stitches. Or bring the thread end to the wrong side and knot it when all of the top-stitching is done. Outline stitch the patterns, leaving no gap between your sewing lines and the edges of the patterns. You may want to slow down when you meet a curve or corner.

5 When all of the top-stitching is done, make sure that the ends of the thread are on the wrong side of the fabric. Then you are ready to proceed to the next step of your project.

5. How to Attach Bias Binding

Bias tape, or bias binding, is frequently used in patchwork projects such as wall hangings or carpets. It is also used when making bags. What follows is an explanation of how to make 3.5 cm bias tapes using a 18 mm tape maker.

How to Make Bias Tapes

This explanation involves a piece of fabric measuring about 1/4 yard (45 cm long × 55 cm wide), because large projects require pieces measuring at least 1/4 yard to 1/2 yard (45 cm long × 110 cm wide). However, ordinary cutting mats are not large enough for this purpose.

❶ Iron the fabric well.

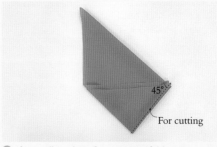

❷ Fold the fabric in half diagonally. The strip of fabric is to be cut on the bevel edge of the triangle.

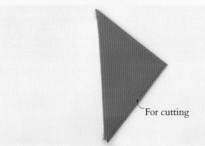

❸ As the edge is too long for your cutting mat and your arm, fold it again at a 45 degree angle, so that the edge is reduced by half.

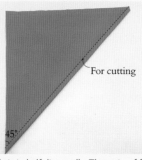

❹ If it is still too long for your mat, fold it one more time, and you will have eight layers of fabric to work with. Generally, this is the limit for your rotary cutter.

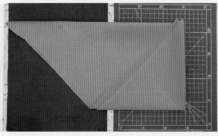

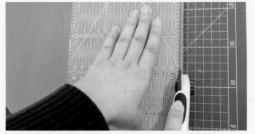

❺ Press the upper edge of the fabric and align it with the line on your mat. Cut a strip from the right edge. You may want to use a ruler to help. With the help of your left thumb and index finger, use your body weight to hold the ruler in place. With the cutter in your right hand, cut from the bottom. Make sure you have cut through all of the layers before your remove your ruler.

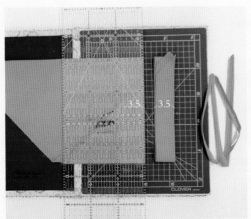

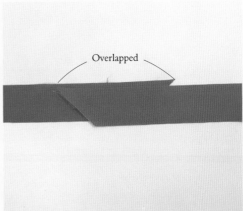

Overlapped

⑥ Cut a strip of 3.5 cm from the right edge. Join the two strips. It is long enough when it is 30 cm longer than the circumference of your project. If it is not, you will need to cut another strip measuring 3.5 cm wide.

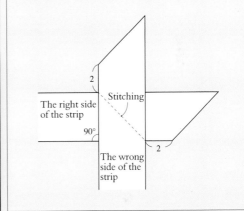

2

Stitching

The right side of the strip

90°

2

The wrong side of the strip

⑦ Place the two strips as shown in the picture, overlapping at one end with 2–3 cm more.

A seam allowance of 0.7 cm

⑧ Sew along the diagonal line of the overlapping square. You may use a guide scrap for back-stitching.

⑨ Trim the seam allowance to 0.7 cm.

⑩ Run your iron along the sewing line. More strips can be joined using this method.

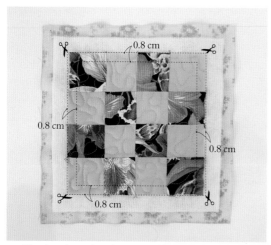 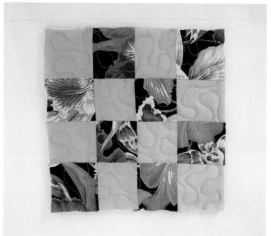

1 The three layers (top, batting, and backing) should be top-stitched together before you wrap the rough edges. Trim around the project using a rotary cutter, so that the seam allowance is 0.8 cm.

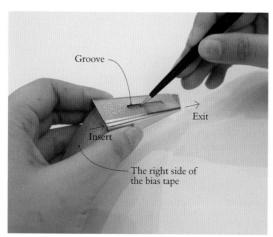 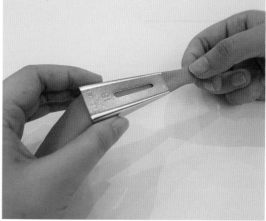

2 With its right side facing you, feed one end of the strip into the wide end of the 18 mm bias tape maker. There's a little groove down the center of the bias tape maker, so you can use a bodkin to pull the fabric through the tape maker if it doesn't slide in easily.

3 Turn the tool over, with the plastic part facing you. Choose the hottest setting on your iron and hold the end of the strip with it. Slowly slide the tape maker along the bias strip for 2–3 cm, until you see that the strip is folded. Move your hot iron along the folded bias to press it well. With your iron on the bias, slide the tape maker for another 2–3 cm, and press it with your iron.

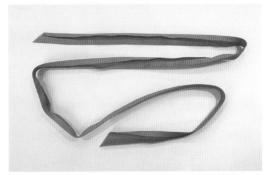

4 Continue to pull and press. When you come to a seam, which is thicker than other places, pull for a short distance or use your fingers to help hold it in place. Be careful not to hurt yourself when using your hand. When the part to be fed is not in a straight line with the tool, the two joining edges will miss the center of the strip.

5 Continue along the entire strip until it has fed completely through the tool.

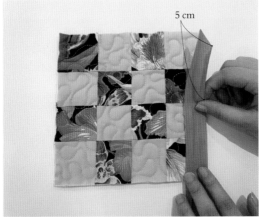

5 cm

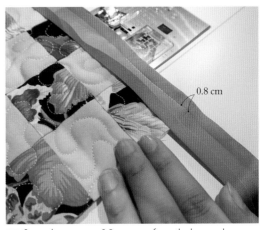

0.8 cm

6 Now it's time to bind. Start in the lower third of the rough edge. Wrap the bias strip around the seam allowances of the fabric, aligning the two right sides together. Stitch along the folding line of the tape, leaving about 5 cm of the end unsewn. Back-stitch at the starting point. Use a straight line for the corner.

7 Stop when you are 0.8 cm away from the lower edge. Back-stitch several times to secure your thread.

45°

Rotate the whole piece 90 degrees

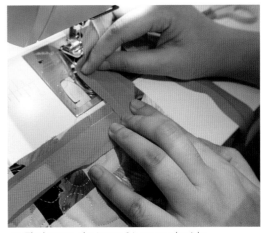

8 Take the whole piece from your machine, and fold the opposite tape around the other edge, lining up the edges. Rotate the whole piece 90 degrees in an anticlockwise direction.

9 The bottom edge in step 8 is now on the right.

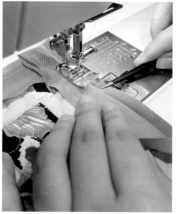

10 Turn the tape over, lining the edges up. Start to sew from the top end of the tape along the folding line until you reach the corner. Repeat what you did. Make sure that you secure your work by back-stitching at the beginning and the end.

11 When all of the four edges are done, you will come to the first one. Stop when you are 15 cm away from where you started.

12 Fold your bias tape triangle up, forming a 45 degree angle. Neatly finger press for a clear line. Trim to a 0.7 seam allowance and securely pin it.

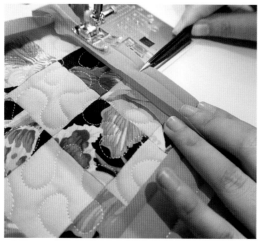

13 Join the two ends and hold them in place with a pin. Continue to sew until you are beyond the meeting area.

14 Back-stitch to secure before your cut off the thread and take the whole piece form the machine.

15 Trim the end to form a 45 degree angle. The tape is now sewn into a circle.

16 Turn the tape to the wrong side of the project.

17 Hide the rough edge along the folding line. Hand sew the tape on the other side onto the backing fabric by using appliqué stitch (see box on page 62). Be sure the stitches on the backing are covered by the tape.

18 Fold a corner into shape before you reach it, as indicated in the picture. Place two stitches on the overlapped area before you continue to work on a different side.

19 Finish all of the sides this way. When you reach the starting point, continue to overlap three or four stitches. Make a knot and insert the needle between the backing fabric and the batting. Exit about 1 cm away and pull the thread slightly to hide the knot between the two. Trim the excessive thread end.

20 You're finished! The picture on the left shows the right side, while the picture on the right shows the wrong side.

Appliqué Stitch

This technique is used to sew a patch onto another piece of fabric, pressing the seam allowance to the wrong side so that it does not show. It is most often used in appliquéing and sewing bias tapes. Generally, thread of a color similar to the appliqué is preferred.

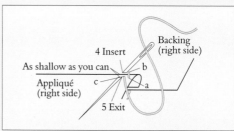

① As shown in the illustration, the first stitch should be done with care so that the knot is hidden between the layers. Where a bias strip is to be sewn, the knot is often between the backing and the bias strip.

② Exit the needle from the edge of the appliqué, but go in as shallow as you can, so that the stitch hardly shows.

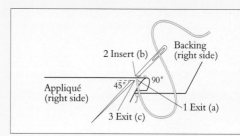

③ Insert the needle vertically to the folded edge of the appliqué (i.e., a straight line between a and b and the folded edge, forming a 90-degree angle in the 1st illustration), but close enough to it so that the stitch does not show. To sew a bias strip, you should penetrate the batting but not the covering fabric, so that the stitch is invisible on the right side of the finished work.

④ Exit 2–3 cm before the first stitch, and go in as shallow as you can. Pull the thread to hide the previous stitch. Continue this way until you reach the end.

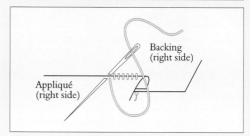

⑤ Make sure that you hide the ending knot between the layers so that it does not show.

6. Embroidery and Beading: The Basics

In embroidery and beading, you "insert" and "exit" your needle. When you insert it, you push it down into the right side of the fabric and come out from the wrong side. When you exit it, you point the needle towards you and insert it through the wrong side of the fabric, and come out from the right side. An embroidery project is done by inserting and exiting your needles.

To embroider a simple line, you can hold the fabric in your hand. However, you will need the help of an embroidery hoop or frame for more complicated designs. For a project no more than 15 cm in diameter, a hand-held circular frame works well; for a piece as large as 20–30 cm, you need a rectangle frame that can be attached to a tabletop. For even larger projects, a freestanding embroidery frame made of four pieces of wood is required. As embroidery and beading are involved in some of the projects in this tutorial, I will explain the basics of the two.

Outline Stitching

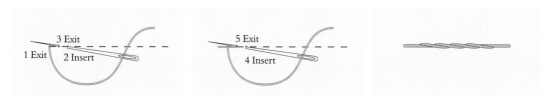

① Thread your needle and knot the end of the thread. Exit the needle at the edge of your pattern and insert it 3 mm away. Don't pull the thread tight, and keep the hoop in place with your thumb. Exit between the two stitches. In the opposite direction, pull the thread firmly, but not so tightly as to make the fabric pucker.

② Insert the needle about 3mm away from the preceding stitch, or 1.5 mm from the second stitch. Don't pull the thread too tightly; press the thread with your thumb. Exit your needle from the hole of the second stitch or at a point close to it. Pull the thread tight.

③ Continue this way until you have a neat line. Make sure that you insert and exit exactly on the mark that you have made. Outline stitching is used for sketching the contours of a pattern in beautifully dense lines, either straight or curved.

Sewing Single Beads

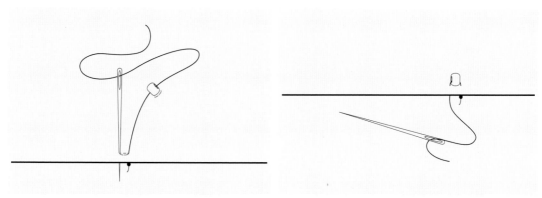

Tie an overhand knot at one end of the thread. Exit from the wrong side of the fabric. Thread a seed bead. Insert your needle into the fabric at a point about the length of the bead. If you prefer a gap between your beads, exit the needle where the next bead will be. Thread the new bead and exit in the direction you choose, with a stitch length of about the length of the bead. Continue this way until the last bead is in place.

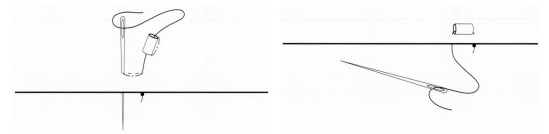

Tube beads are stitched in a similar way: Exiting from the wrong side of the fabric, thread a tube bead. Insert your needle into the fabric at a point about the length of the bead. When you prefer a gap between your beads, exit the needle where the next bead will be. Thread the new bead and exit in the direction you choose, with a stitch length of about the length of the bead. Continue this way until the last bead is in place.

Sewing Combinations for Seed Beads

 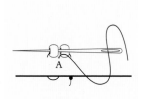 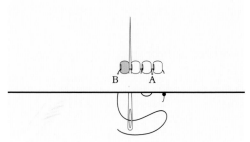

① Tie an overhand knot at one end of the thread. Exit from the wrong side of the fabric. Thread two seed beads. Insert your needle into the fabric at a point about the length of two beads.

② Exit the needle at point A between the beads. Thread a new bead and pull the thread through.

③ Re-thread the two beads. Work forward and insert the needle at point B. Your stitch length is now the gap between A and B, or the length of three beads. Exit between the last two beads and through the second one (the leftmost one in the picture). Thread two new beads and continue until your last beads are in place. If you have more beads to be stitched, you may prefer threading four beads at a time, and back-stitching over two of them, or threading six and back-stitching over three.

Sewing Combinations for Tube Beads

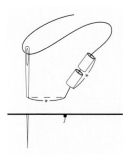 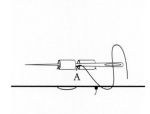 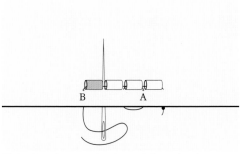

① Exit where your first bead will be. Thread two tube beads. Insert your needle into the fabric at a point about the length of two beads.

② Exit the needle at point A between the beads. Re-thread the second bead and pull the thread through.

③ Re-thread two new beads. Work forward and insert the needle at point B. Your stitch length is now the gap between A and B, or the length of three tube beads. Exit between the last two added beads and through the second one (the leftmost one in the picture). Thread two new beads and continue until your last beads are in place. If your bead is longer than 6 mm, you are suggested to work with a maximum of four at a time, and back-stitch two of them.

Sewing a Sequin on One Side

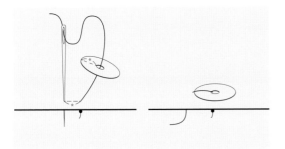 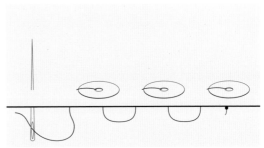

To stitch a flat sequin, exit your needle where the sequin is supposed to be fastened. Thread a sequin. Position it where you choose, about half of the sequin away. Sequins can be flat or cupped. The former is often used separately, and the latter goes with beads.

If you prefer a gap between your sequins, exit the needle where the next sequin will be. Thread a new one and exit in the direction you choose, with a stitch length of about half of the sequin. Continue this way until the last piece is done.

Sewing a Sequin on Two Sides

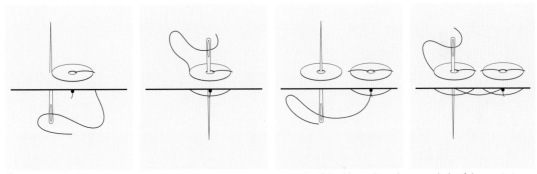

① Tie an overhand knot at one end of the thread. Exit from the wrong side of the fabric where the center hole of the sequin is supposed to be. Thread a sequin. Insert your needle into the fabric on one side of the sequin, at a point about half of the sequin away from the first stitch.

② Exit your third stitch close to the opposite edge of the sequin. Then insert the needle into its center hole.

③ Exit from the hole in a new sequin when necessary.

④ Repeat step 2.

Fastening Sequins

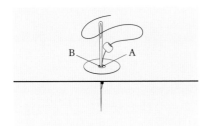 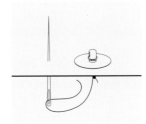 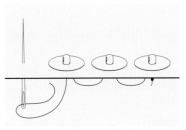

① Tie an overhand knot at one end of the thread. Exit from the wrong side of the fabric where the center hole of the sequin is supposed to be (point A). Thread a bead and a sequin, and then insert your needle into the center hole again at point B.

② Fasten the bead and the sequin onto the fabric.

③ Repeat this when a new bead or sequin is to be sewed.

Fig. 28 The Wall Hanging of the *Three and All* Series (detail)
Please refer to pages 106–107.

CHAPTER 5
Gallery

I fell in love with patchwork when I was trying to craft a make-up bag. Just like many other lovers of this art form, I followed the steps in a book. Since then, I have flung myself into it, making more and more lovely household items, all of which are easy to do. This chapter displays some examples, including a carefully designed handbag, a mouse pad made from random leftover pieces of fabric, a lovely collecting bag, and a fashionable iPad case. Featuring Chinese culture, these designs have a distinctly Asian flavor.

1. Peach Blossom Garden (Mouse Pad)

Patchwork lovers end up with tons of leftover pieces of fabric. Instead of wasting them, why not save them for small projects? Over the years, I have enjoyed recycling my loose fabric scraps in crazy ways that are fun and easy to do.

As an example, I will explain how I created a patchwork mouse pad. It is named after an essay by the well-known poet Tao Yuanming (352 or 365–427) from the Eastern Jin dynasty (317–420), which tells the story of a peaceful and quiet life in a fairyland full of grass and flowers.

Leftover fabric with patterns of trees and flowers were chosen for the design, to create a spring-like atmosphere. Two pieces of pink were added, giving the impression of a far-away hill covered with blooming peach trees or a sky with layers of cloud. Fabric scraps of different colors are matched to express the theme.

Supplies

Completed size: 23 × 23 cm
Fabric scraps: various colors and
   sizes
Adhesive batting: 25 × 25 cm
Backing fabric: 25 × 25 cm
Thread: machine embroidery
   thread

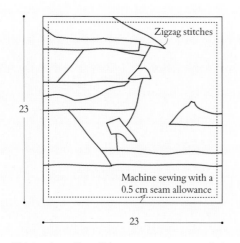

1 This is a demo. You will have to create your own designs according to the colors and shapes of your leftovers.

2 Pick larger pieces of different colors, shapes, and patterns that you think will work well in your design. Iron them for later use. Be sure to prepare more varieties than you will use.

3 Some smaller scraps are also needed for decorative purposes.

4 Cut out a 25 × 25 cm piece of one-sided adhesive batting. Choose a patch with patterns that will dominate the design and place it on the adhesive side of the batting. You can cut a piece into any shape you like, but make sure it has a trimmed raw edge.

5 Place another piece with an overlap of 2–3 mm.

6 Add more patches with the same overlapping. Make sure the added layer is about 3–5 mm larger than the batting on the four sides.

7 The orders of the added pieces can be adjusted according to the overall design, rather than when they are added. Continue until the batting is fully covered and you are satisfied with the design.

8 Run a warm iron over the right side until the leftovers are fixed stably to the batting.

 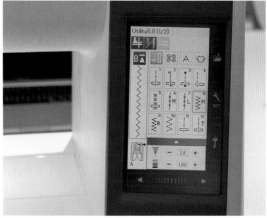

9 Zigzag stitch on your machine along each joining line to hold them together. Before you start, you may want to try a different fabric for your favorite stitch length and density. Silk embroidery thread of the dominant colors of the design is recommended.

10 When small decorative pieces are placed on top of other pieces and cannot be stabilized on the batting, put them aside temporarily. Pin them securely before sewing them onto the work when the others are in place.

11 Trim the edges to the size of the batting material.

12 Cut out a patch of backing fabric of 25 × 25 cm and iron it well. Place it exactly over your finished patchwork. Pin them together securely. Stitch along each edge with a 1 cm seam, leaving an opening of 10 cm to turn the inside out. Remember to back-stitch at the beginning and end of stitching. Trim the edge to about 0.5 cm.

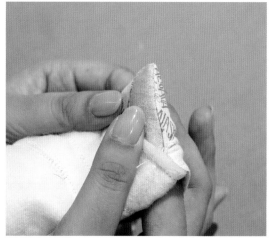

13 Remove the pins. Turn the inside out. For a professional finished appearance at the corners, you may fold the corner at a 90-degree angle using your fingers.

14 Fold the edges inward around the opening. Iron the area to stabilize it.

15 Close the opening using blind stitches (i.e., ladder stitch or invisible stitch).

16 Run an iron over the right side. Top-stitching along the edge, 0.5 cm away from the edge.

17 Sit back and enjoy your creation!

2. *First Snow* (iPad Case)

This project, while machine-made like the one before, is dramatically different in color combination. It owes its inspiration to three rolls of fabric stacked on top of one another: a white one with paint-like dye, a blue-gray one with white dots that look like water drops or flecks of snow, and a grayish-white one with Van Gogh-like patterns. They remind me of snow-covered mountains and a blue sky, like a Chinese ink-and-watsh painting. This project features simple colors, but the use of space and fabric with Roman lettering lend it a modern flavor.

Supplies

Completed size: 20 × 15 cm
Fabric scraps: various colors and
   sizes
Adhesive batting: 30 × 45 cm
Inside pocket fabric: 30 × 40 cm

Strap for fastener: 10 cm
Button or bead as button: 1
   (optional)
Thread: machine embroidery thread
Tassel: 1 (optional)

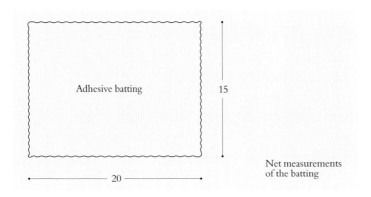

Adhesive batting

15

20

Net measurements
of the batting

1 Pick fabric pieces of different colors, shapes, and patterns that work for your design. Iron them for later use. Cut two patches of adhesive batting of the size marked in the diagrams, for the front and the back of your case.

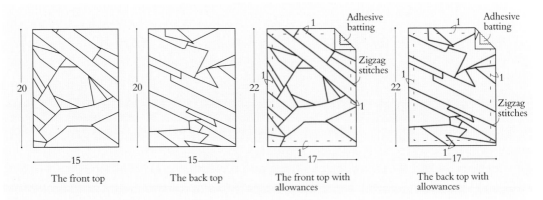

The front top   The back top   The front top with allowances   The back top with allowances

2 Arrange your scraps on the batting in whichever combinations of colors and patterns you like. Iron them so that they are held securely in place. Select the zigzag stitch on your machine and sew each of them onto the batting. When you have finished, trim the seam allowances so that they are 1 cm larger than the batting on each side. You might want to refer back to the more detailed instructions for the mouse pad. For demonstration purposes, the iPad used here is 17 cm wide × 24 cm high, and the case is designed to be 1 cm larger in length and width than the machine. If yours is different, measure its dimensions and add 1–2 cm all around.

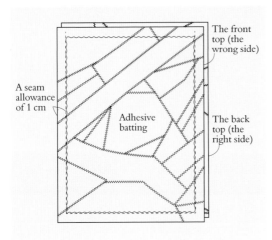

3 Lay your two pieces of material out, with their right sides together. Sew along all the edges but the top. Turn the right side out.

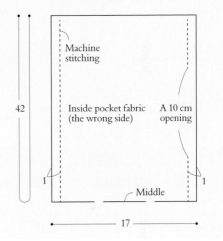

4 Mark your inside pocket fabric for sewing lines, leaving an allowance of 1 cm. Fold the material in half, with the right sides together. Sew along the two sewing lines, leaving a 10 cm opening on one side to turn it out.

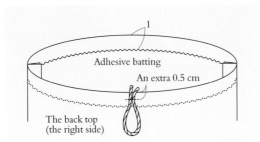

5 Hand sew your fastener onto the center of the front of the outside layer (top), with the ring part downward, leaving an extra 0.5 cm between your sewing line and the edge. A ring the size of a button is needed for your fastener. Trim it, leaving a 1 cm tail.

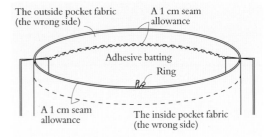

6 Match the inside pocket fabric with the right side of the outside pocket fabric, and hold them in place with pins on both sides and in the middle. Sew around the edge on your machine. Turn the right side out. Make the bottom corner into a perfect arc, and sew up the opening using drawing stitches. Run a warm iron over it. You now have a cute case for your iPad!

3. *Life* (Collecting Bag)

This project features a tiger and bamboo. The former is "the monarch of all beasts" in traditional Chinese culture. The latter, together with the plum, orchid, and chrysanthemum, is a metaphor for a Chinese gentleman, who is supposed to be modest, self-disciplined, and indifferent to fame and wealth. On the front side is a majestic tiger prowling around its territory during the daytime. The other side features bamboo branches, between which smoke and moon light are seen, as if a gentleman is on his way home in the evening. The moving tiger forms a sharp contrast with the quiet bamboo forest. The colors beige and light blue dominate the design, to give an air of peace and quietness.

Supplies

Completed size: 20.5×15.5 cm
Fabric scraps: various colors and sizes
Adhesive batting: 50×25 cm
Inside pocket fabric: 50×25 cm

Hanging straps: 100 cm
Thread: bobbin thread, top-stitching thread of colors maching the fabric scraps

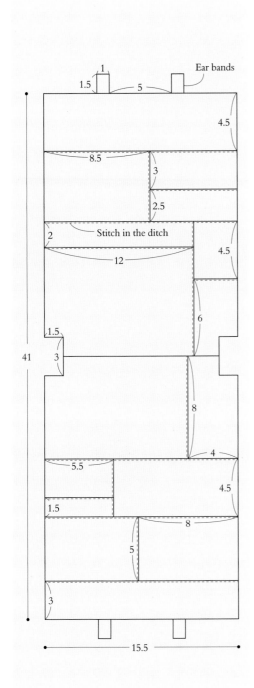

The diagram shows measurements:

1
1.5
5   Ear bands
4.5
8.5
3
2.5
2   Stitch in the ditch
12
4.5
6
1.5
3
8
4
5.5
4.5
1.5
8
5
3
41
15.5

2 When your scraps have the same fiber orientation, place them upwards; otherwise, arrange them in any manner you like. The arrangements in the picture are suggestions, and can be adjusted according to your design and the order of the machine work.

A		I	
B	C	J	K
	D	L	M
E			N
F	G	O	P
	H		

The Front   The Back

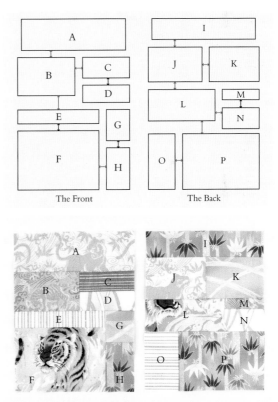

1 Cut two patches for the front and the back of the bag. Choose fabric in your favorite colors and patterns. The measurements indicated are net, and seam allowances should be maintained for hand or machine stitching.

3 Stitch the patches together in the order indicated (please refer to the colors of the arrows). The black ones mean the pieces should be stitched at first, the red ones secondly and the purple ones thirdly. The seam allowances should be pressed in the direction of the piece with the darker color. In machine stitching, run an iron along an allowance before you start to work on a new piece, to avoid unsatisfactory finish seams.

Stitches

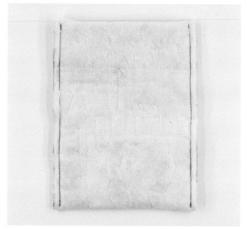

5 Fold the whole patch along the middle line, with the right sides together. Stitch along the right and left edges.

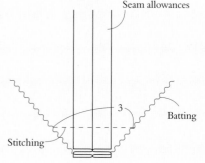

Seam allowances

3

Batting

Stitching

4 When the front and back pieces are ready, place one on top of the other with the right sides together. Make sure that they orient the same direction, so that your bag has the right patterns on both sides. Start machine stitching from the bottom. Cut a patch of adhesive batting of 42.5 × 17 cm and paste it to the back of the top with a warm iron. Run your machine along the seams to hold them together. You might also want to add top-stitching to outline the patterns on a couple of larger scraps, which can also help to hold the fabric and batting together.

6 Open the bag all the way to the bottom and poke out the corners. Stitch about 3 cm of the bottom together, trim the seam allowances, and reduce bulk.

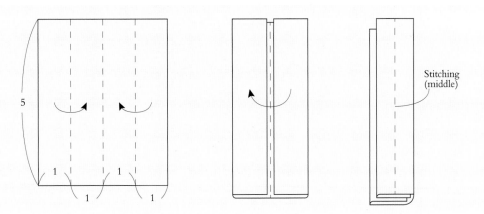

7 Cut 5 × 4 cm scraps for four ear bands. They can be of the same material you have used for the body of the bag, or fabric from a different category or pattern. Fold each in half lengthwise. Turn both edges to the middle, and then fold it again to form a 5×1 cm strap. Sew the strap in the middle.

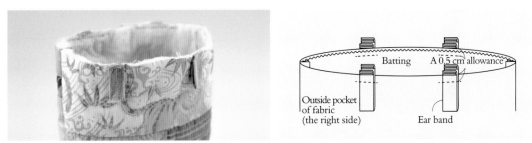

8 Fold each ear band in half and fasten it to the bag with a pin or clip, lining its rough edge up with that of the bag. Stitch them together, with an allowance of no more than 0.7 cm. To secure your straps, you may want to start and end your stitching somewhere away from the edges of the strap.

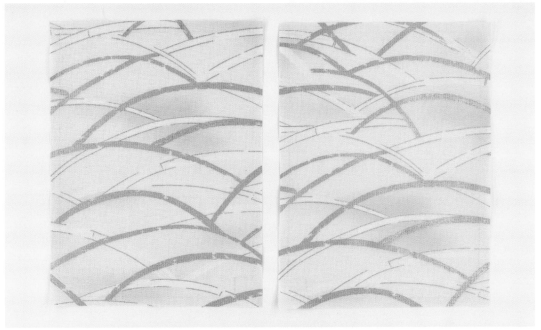

9 Now switch to the inside pocket of fabric, which is made from two pieces of 22 × 17 cm. Make sure they are oriented with the patterns facing upwards. As stitching reduces the size of your outside pocket fabric, it is important to match the two layers. Where fiber orientation is not considered, you may prefer to use one piece measuring 42.5 × 17 cm and skip the next step.

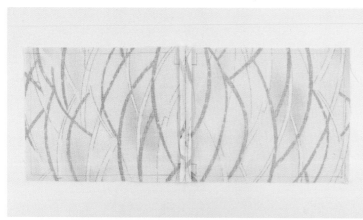

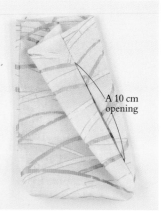

A 10 cm
opening

10 Sew the two pieces with their right sides together, and press the seam on both sides. As you did in step 5, fold the cloth in half lengthwise. Sew along the left and right edges, leaving a 10 cm opening in the middle (rather than at the starting point) on one side to turn it out. Repeat what you did in step 6, opening the bag all the way to the bottom to poke out the corners, stitching about 3 cm of the bottom together, and reducing bulk.

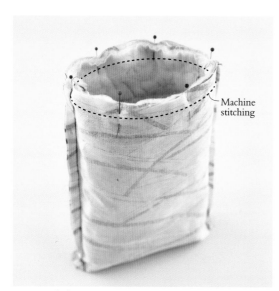

Machine
stitching

11 With the wrong side of the inside pocket fabric and the right side of the outside pocket fabric facing you, put the outside one into the inside one. Line up the seams of the two layers and hold them together with pins. Press the allowances on both sides to reduce thickness. The bag shown on the right has its opening finished.

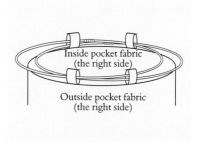

Inside pocket fabric
(the right side)

Outside pocket fabric
(the right side)

12 Turn the right side out and sew up the opening. The opening can be finished by machine or by hand. The difference is that blind stitching by hand leaves no trace. When a machine is used, the allowance is tucked into the inside layer and the opening is stitched 0.1–0.2 cm inside the edge. Thread of similar color to the inside pocket fabric is recommended.

13 Thread your hanging strap into place, then enjoy your bag!

4. Cat and Chinese Rose (Appliquéd Shirt)

The rose has been important in the cultivation of garden plants in China for more than two thousand years, and is regarded as "the queen of flowers." I grow Chinese roses in my garden, and I love to watch my cat enjoying herself among the blooms.

This project involves appliquéing a shirt, but you can use the skills in all sorts of fabric projects, such as decorating a pair of jeans, a purse, or even pillow shams. Instead of following a design, I tend to just wing it, making full use of the scraps I have and the patterns on them. With a little imagination you can be just as creative.

Supplies

A white shirt with a pocket
Fabric scraps: various colors and sizes
Tear-away stabilizer: the size of a sheet of A4 paper
Thread: machine embroidery thread

1 Pick some fabric scraps with plant and flower patterns, and iron them well. Cut the stabilizer into pieces that are larger than the plants and flowers, and press them onto the wrong side of the patterns with a warm iron. Cut out all of the pattern pieces. You may choose to appliqué a cat using the pattern on your small scraps, or a cat transferred from a paper pattern with the size you prefer. To do the latter, transfer a paper pattern of a cat onto the wrong side of the stabilizer, and cut it out with a 2–3 mm added to the size all round. Press the pattern onto the wrong side of a piece of black fabric, or fabric in your favorite color. Cut it out. Do the same with the ears and the white parts of the eyes. Of course, you can choose any other animal. Just follow the same procedure.

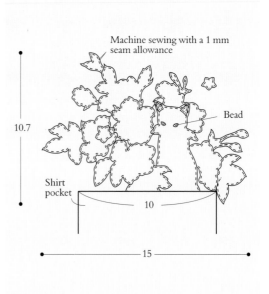

Machine sewing with a 1 mm
seam allowance

Bead

10.7

Shirt
pocket

10

15

2 Play with the design, moving the pieces of the cat and the
plants until you come upon a pleasing arrangement. Take a
picture of your design. Tear off the stabilizers, starting from the
one at the bottom, and press the pattern pieces one by one
onto your shirt with a warm iron.

3 Machine sew the pieces with straight stitches 1–1.5 mm
away from the edges. For a better finish, adjust your stitch
density from 2 mm to 1.8 mm.

4 You may want to highlight the flowers and leaves using threads of different colors. This also helps to hold the patterns in place.
Add the eyes by embroidering or beading, and you're finished.

5. *Dunhuang Landscape* (Appliquéd Notebook Cover)

Two of the most striking fabrics in my collection are a marine-themed piece, and a skein with grass patterns that resemble the designs of William Morris (1834–1896)—a British textile designer associated with the British Arts and Crafts Movement. The lotus and bird patterns remind me of the Chinese desert city of Dunhuang on the Silk Road, which was an ancient network of trade routes that connected the East to the West.

This project features the colors of the sea and the desert, with the mysterious Morris-style patterns in between, showing how the land and waterway trade routes complemented each other to create a better world.

Supplies

Completed size: 27.5 × 25.5 cm
Covering fabric scraps: various
  colors and sizes
Backing fabric: 65 × 35 cm

Medium weight interlining: 65 × 35 cm
Thin interlining: 65 × 35 cm
Notebook with a hard cover:
  18 × 22 × 1.5 cm

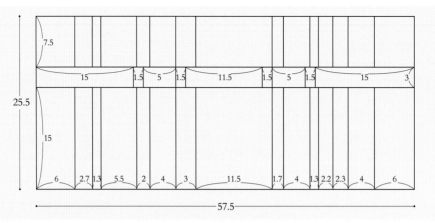

1 Pick your favorite fabric and cut out the blocks according to your paper patterns for machine sewing. Arrange them as shown in the diagram. The measurements will vary depending on the size of your notebook.

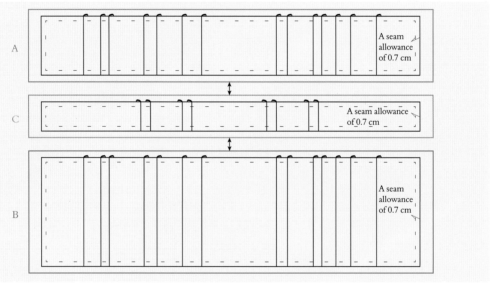

2 Piece the blocks together using the techniques introduced in Machine Sewing (Blocks of Different Sizes) (page 45). Stitch sections A and C first, and piece them with section B.

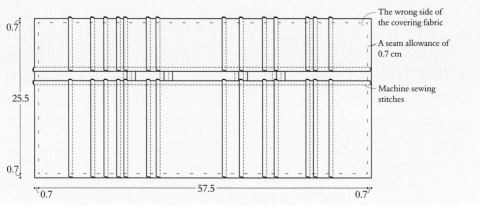

3 The seam allowances between sections A and B share the same direction, but those in section C are pressed in the opposite direction. The seam allowances at the top and at the bottom are pressed towards section C.

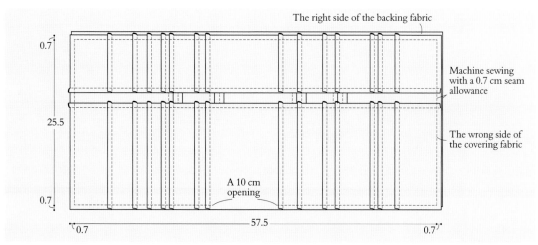

The right side of the backing fabric

0.7

25.5

Machine sewing with a 0.7 cm seam allowance

The wrong side of the covering fabric

A 10 cm opening

0.7

0.7

57.5

0.7

4 Draw 59 × 27 cm blocks on the medium weight and thin interlinings and cut them out. Using a warm iron, press the covering fabric onto the medium weight one and the backing fabric onto the thin one. With right sides together, machine sew along the edges of the block, leaving an opening of 10 cm at the bottom.

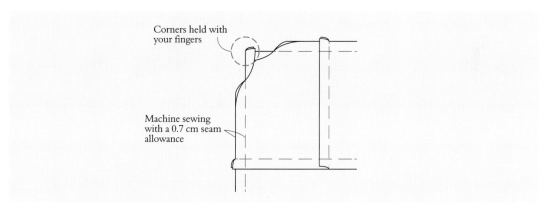

Corners held with your fingers

Machine sewing with a 0.7 cm seam allowance

5 Turn the right side out. Fold the corners and hold them with your fingers to finish the corners neatly. Iron the cover flat, and sew the opening using blind stitches.

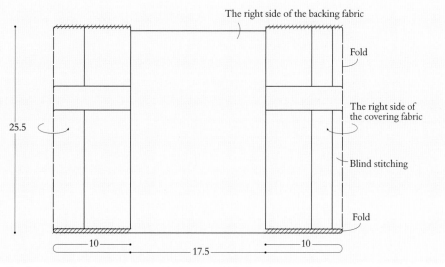

The right side of the backing fabric

Fold

The right side of the covering fabric

25.5

Blind stitching

Fold

10

17.5

10

6 With the backing facing you, fold 5 cm of the two sides into the middle. Sew the top and the bottom of the overlapping parts with blind stitches.

6. *Four Seasons* (Handbags)

In Chinese culture, flowers, rocks, and wood have metaphysical meanings for men of letters. Traditional *gongbi* paintings of branches with flowers, especially by artists in Song dynasty, have long been considered among the best for their gorgeous lines, lifelike images, and artistic conceptions. These painting techniques can be employed in patchwork, to create an effect rarely seen in mainstream projects. This handbag project, named *Four Seasons*, features a flower or plant for each season.

For demonstrative purposes, the *Heavenly Bamboo* bag is shown in a step-by-step tutorial, while other three flowers are represented in the appliquéing processes as explained in images and diagrams. The conceptions and designs of the project are also laid out.

Winter: Heavenly Bamboo

Heavenly bamboo flowers are small and white, and bloom from March to June in conical clusters. The fruits are bright red berries, which often persist through the winter.

Painters in ancient China liked to feature bonsai trees with different "lucky" flowers in their work, to celebrate the coming of the spring and the new year. Heavenly bamboo was among their favorites. When creating this project, I was inspired by several traditional paintings, in addition to my own observations.

Supplies

Completed size: height 25 cm, width 32 cm, bottom width 6 cm

Outside pocket fabric: printed fabric cut to 100 × 40 cm

Fabric scraps: fabric patches in different colors

Inside pocket fabric: printed fabric cut to 90 × 35 cm

Medium weight interlining: 90 × 70 cm

Adhesive batting: 90 × 35 cm

Beads and sequins of different colors

Thread: multi-colored bobbin thread (for top-stitching and sewing beads)

Metal frame: 25 cm

1 Cut your fabric according to the paper patterns of the template, and complete the appliquéing on your machine. Cut four copies of the interlining according to the template, two of which have a seam allowance of 1 cm, and two of which have net measurements. Iron a piece with an allowance to the wrong side of the outside pocket fabric for the front of the handbag, to which you will add a piece without an allowance. In the same way, iron the other two pieces to the wrong side of the outside pocket fabric for the back of the handbag.

Transfer the life-sized pattern onto the adhesive batting. Cut two copies. Place one on the wrong sides of both the front piece and the back piece. Top-stitch the front piece around the pattern edge and sew your beads onto it. Your beads may be different, and they can be sewn however you like.

Template

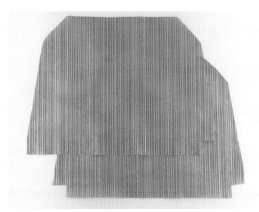

2 Transfer the life-sized pattern onto the inside pocket fabric. Cut two copies with a seam allowance of 1 cm.

3 Pin the front and back pieces of the outside fabric in the bottom center, with the right sides together. Stitch along the middle line, starting and ending about 3–5 mm away from the edge, so that they are held together securely. Trim the seam, leaving a 0.7 cm allowance. Finish the inside pocket fabric this way.

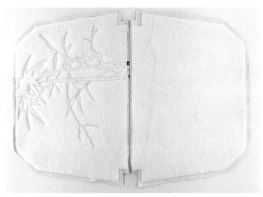

4 Press the seam allowance open. Do the same with the inside pocket fabric.

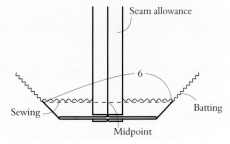

5 Fold the outside fabric in half along the middle line. Pin the two sides and stitch down, starting from the upward end, but end 3–5mm away from the other end. The upward end is where the outside pocket fabric and the inside pocket fabric will be stitched together, so overdoing it will affect the finished shape of your bag. Do the same with the inside pocket fabric.

6 Fold the opening part at the lower left corner in half in the direction perpendicular to the surface of the bag, so that the intersection points in steps 3 and 5 are aligned. Stitch them together. Do the same with the opening part at the lower right corner, forming a 6 cm-wide bottom. Do the same with the inside pocket fabric.

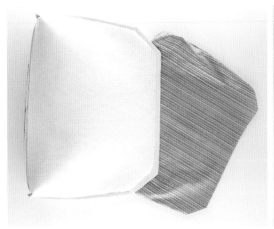
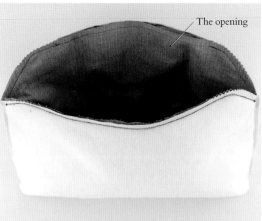

The opening

7 Put the inside pocket into the cover bag, with the right side of the former and the wrong side of the latter facing you. Make sure that the side openings of the two are lined up. Hold the two in place with pins on one side, and sew them together. Be sure to avoid stitching the seam allowances. Then do the same with the other side, but leave a 15–20 cm opening on the straight part.

8 Trim the seam allowance to 0.7 cm. Pinking scissors are the best choice, but general-purpose ones work as well. Cut the four curved parts into wavy cuts, so that the corners are not too thick when you turn the right side out.

9 Turn the right side out. It is easier if you start with one bottom corner before the rest is taken inside out. Make sure that the corners and the upper edges are in the desired shapes.

10 Hold the openings in place with pins. Sew them together about 0.2–0.3 cm away from the opening of the bag, leaving at least 3 cm from the bottom at the beginning and ending points.

11 Take your metal frame and insert one side of the bag into it. Make sure that the two fit well. The distance between the two bottom ends of the bag and the frame are good reference points. Use thread to hold the two in place temporarily, as seen in the picture.

12 Knot your hand sewing thread at the end. Exit your needle from the first hole and insert it into the bottom of the second. The thread can be thin leather or top-stitching thread, and one strand is strong enough for the frame. Two strands are recommended if hand sewing thread is used. The color of the machine thread should match the outside pocket fabric.

13 Exit from the top of the second hole, and insert the needle at the bottom of the third hole.

 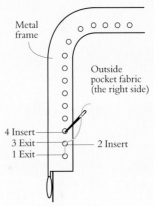

14 Repeat step 13 until one side of the frame is finished. Remove the temporary fastening thread. Do the same with the other side. This method is preferable, because the stitches are dotted rather than linear, and it is tough enough.

15 Iron the outside pocket fabric flat again. Make sure your bag is in perfect shape, and you're done!

Spring: Chinese Plum

The flowering of the Chinese plum in late winter and early spring is regarded as a seasonal symbol. In one of his poems, Chen Liang (1143–1194), a poet in the Song dynasty, praised the tree for being first to announce the coming of spring. As one of the most beloved flowers in China, the plum blossom has been frequently depicted in Chinese art and poetry for many centuries. The blossoms are so popular because they bloom vibrantly in the snow, and as such symbolize perseverance, purity, and independence.

This project aims to impress by the freshness and elegance created by the thin branches and buds of the plum, in sharp contrast with the young bamboo.

Template

Summer: Lotus

The lotus is an aquatic plant that blossoms in summer, between June and September. It has been a popular flower in Chinese literature, painting, and art, because "while growing from mud, it is unstained," as Zhou Dunyi (1017–1073), a Neo-Confucianist of the Northern Song dynasty (960–1127) wrote in one of his essays.

For this project, I chose a main fabric that looks like the wavy surface of lake water. The soft petals of the flower are made of a printed fabric from my favorite collection, which makes the outside fabric look like a Chinese ink-and-wash painting. As the lotus leaves are very large, some beads and sequins were added. They highlight a change of color, and look like dewdrops.

Template

Fall: Crape Myrtle

When I think of flowers in fall, what immediately springs to mind is the crape myrtle tree with its colorful flowers in conical clusters. I got the inspiration for this project from a painting of a crape myrtle by Song dynasty artist Wei Sheng (dates unknown). I attempted to recreate the clear lines of *gongbi* and the freedom of freehand brush work, while keeping the background as simple as I could. Beads were used for the small flowers.

Template

7. Peach Blossom (Appliquéd Frame)

Chinese landscape painting has a special category called "green-and-blue landscape," which features pigments made from the minerals azurite and malachite. This project owes its inspiration to this unique style, and features peach blossoms as the highlight.

Supplies

Completed size: 27 cm (diameter)
White backing fabric: 45 × 45 cm
Fabric scraps: various colors and sizes

Tracing paper: 35 × 35 cm
Tear-away stabilizer:
    45 × 45 cm

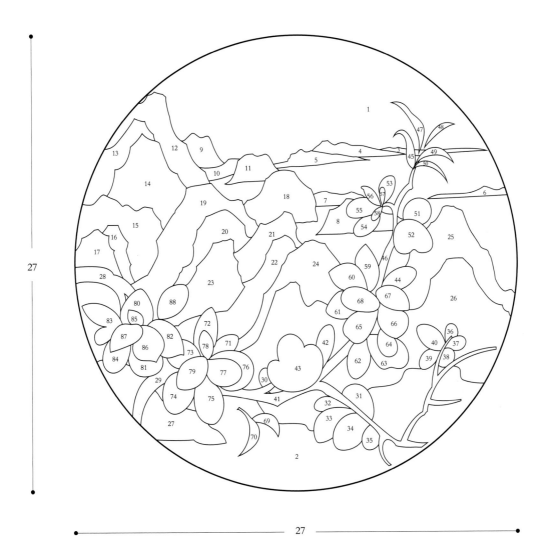

27

27

Template

1 Transfer the paper patterns of the template onto the
tracing paper and number each of them.

2 Cut the fabric scraps and finish the appliqué work with the
stabilizer and your iron, using techniques of appliquéing by
machine (page 48).

3 Lockstitch the edges of the covering fabric, using steps
15–16 in appliquéing by machine. You may choose not to
lockstitch, as a frame is needed when it is finished.

4 Leave the excess backing fabric as it is, and have it
mounted. The size of the frame will vary according to
your needs. A piece of white cardboard with a hole of 27 cm
diameter in the center is needed on top of the finished work
to hide the rough edge.

8. Lucky Clouds (Mat)

In the mythologies of many cultures, mysterious immortal beings live high in the clouds. Chinese tradition is no exception, and the cloud is considered to be lucky in China. Cloud patterns are often visible in Chinese paintings, frescoes, and costumes. These patterns are highly decorative and come in many attractive varieties. When I was creating this project, the image of clouds sprang to mind.

Appliqué stitch is used to finish the covering for the project, because it helps hide the stitches and offers a better finish for the clouds. Of course, machine stitching works as well.

Supplies

Completed size: 100 × 61.5 cm
Background fabric: 110 × 70 cm
Fabric scraps: various colors and sizes
Backing fabric: 130 × 90 cm
Batting: 120 × 80 cm

Tracing paper: 110 × 70 cm
Freezer paper as needed
Thread: hand-sewing thread and
    machine embroidery thread

Template with drawing of stitches in the ditch

Illustration with the order of appliquéing

1 Make a copy of the template as it is. Trace the patterns on tracing paper and outline the frame. Number them.

2 Turn the tracing paper over. With the shiny side of the freezer paper facing down, lay it on the tracing paper. Trace each pattern on the dull side of the freezer paper in order. Make sure that you are as accurate as possible.

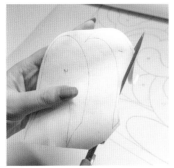

3 Number each pattern on the freezer paper and cut it out.

4 Pick your fabric, and iron it flat. With the wrong side of the fabric and the shiny side of the freezer paper together, run a warm iron over them so that they stick together. Cut the fabric out using a seam allowance of 5 mm.

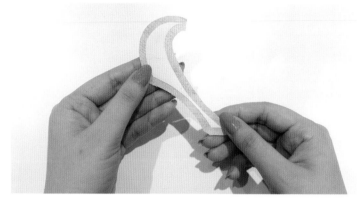

5 Once all the patches are done, cut the background fabric to 105 × 66.5 cm. Transfer the design onto the background fabric with an erasable pen.

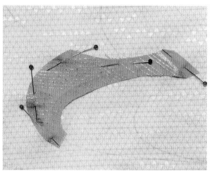

6 Now start your appliqué work with patch No.1. Match it with its outline on the backgound fabric and pin it up. As the four outer edges of the patch are to be covered by other patches, you don't have to sew it. Simply pin it up.

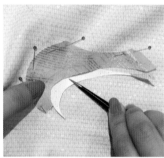

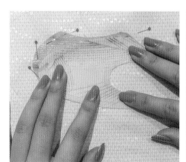

7 Separate the freezer paper and the fabric with a needle. Pull the freezer paper out using a pair of tweezers.

8 Iron freezer paper No.2 to the wrong side of the fabric and cut it out with a seam allowance of 5 mm. Match it with its outline on the backgound fabric and pin it up.

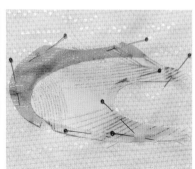

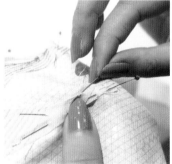

9 Fold the seam allowance inward and sew the patch to the background using appliqué stitch (page 62). Work only on the parts of the pattern that will be visible when finished, leaving the invisible parts as they are.

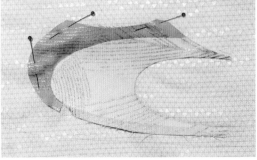

10 Fine cuts are needed for sewing a curve. The cuts should be 2 mm away from the freezer paper. Where the seam allowance is too much, cut it to 3 mm.

Tips for Appliquéing Stitching

❶ Appliquéing stitching always starts from the lowest layer, so the parts that are to be covered by following layers are often left unsewn. A large enough unsewn part can be used as the opening to remove the freezer paper.

❷ For a patch with a closed pattern, a gentle curve is the best starting point. When you are about 2–3 cm away from where you start, fold the remaining seam allowance inward and iron it well so that you have a clear edge. Separate the freezer paper and pull it out. Sew up the opening.

❸ When you are working on a patch as long as patch No.5 (see page 101), the above method will not work so well. Instead, sew a long edge first, tear off the freezer paper, and pull it out every 5 cm when you are working on the other long edge.

11 Sew the patches in the order shown in the illustration with the order of appliquéing to finish the covering. Iron the covering fabric well, and trace the pattern to be stiched with an erasable pen. Place the covering, the batting, and the backing on top of each other and sew them up using stitches in the ditch (page 54). Where there is enough space, a freestyle stitching can be more creative, as shown in the above illustration. Trim the edges with a rotary cutter. Bind the raw edges with bias tapes (page 56) and you're done.

Fig. 29 The Carpet of the *Shanglin Garden* Series (detail)
Please refer to pages 142–144.

CHAPTER 6
Creative Patchwork Series

This chapter introduces more complicated projects: the *Three and All* and the *Shanglin Garden*. These two projects focus on the household, with a tablecoth, carpets, cushions, and thin blankets to match the wall hangings. The wall hangings take the form of a set of Chinese paintings, displaying a full scene in independent but related parts.

While a step-by-step procedure is explained for each project with life-sized templates, my conceptions of them are shared. Due to the overall design and fabric choices, these complicated projects are not to be duplicated, but they can serve as references for creative projects of your own.

1. The *Three and All* Series

This project aims to decorate a simple dining room space with the help of a landscape created by wall hangings, a tablecloth, a carpet, cushions, and a thin blanket. The wall hangings echo the grassland, slopes, and flowers outside the window, featuring different shades of green to represent nature. The tablecloth looks like a bubbling stream in the moonlight, while the cushions, and the blanket are adorned with banks of wild flowers.

As I was working on the project, I often thought of Laozi's words in the *Dao De Jing*: "Dao generates one, one generates two, two generates three, and three generates all." What a patchwork contains is physically limited, but the composition creates an endless space and entails infinite variation, which represent the artist's love and respect for life and nature; hence, the title "Three and All."

What follows is an explanation of a part of the work. The wall hangings are three individual pieces of 200 × 67 cm, resembling a set of vertical Chinese paintings. The composition is somewhat complicated, so only the part featuring plantains in the third piece is explained here as an individual work.

Wall Hanging

1 Make a copy of the template as it is.

2 Cut the tracing paper so that it is 2 cm larger all round than the pattern, and transfer the pattern onto it. Number each piece as it is in the composition. Make sure the outline is traced as well.

3 Turn over the tracing paper. Starting from No.1 in Section A, transfer each piece onto the stabilizer and cut it out, leaving enough seam allowance. Refer to appliquéing by machine (page 48) when needed in the following steps.

4 Match each fabric piece with the corresponding pattern on the stabilizer and cut it out. Number them so that you can identify them.

5 Lay a high-density foam mattress on the worktable and spread the well-ironed white or light colored fabric on it. Hold them in place with pins at the edge. With the right side of the tracing paper facing you, place it on the fabric. Pin the patterns onto the fabric.

6 Iron the pieces onto the background fabric in the order indicated.

7 Remove the covering fabric and tear off the tracing paper. Machine appliqué the pieces using an embroidery thread of the color matching the pattern. Handle the covering fabric with care to stop the surface from piling.

8 When you finish the appliqué work, place the backing, the batting, and the covering on top of one another. Hold the three layers in place with safety pins, and sew along the edges of each pattern using stitching in the ditch (page 54). Where there is enough blank space, you may want to be more creative and use freestyle stitching.

9 Trim the tracing paper and place it on top of the stitched project, lining up the edges. Outline the design using a water or air erasable pen. As the stitched work is somewhat smaller, trim the three layers with a rotary cutter along a line about 0.8 cm away from the contours.

10 Make bias tapes using a 3.5 cm strip (page 56) and finish all the raw edges.

Supplies

Completed size: 117 × 60 cm
Background fabric: white or light colored
   cotton fabric cut to 123 × 65 cm
Fabric scraps: various colors and sizes
General-purpose batting: 133 × 75 cm
Backing fabric: 143 × 85 cm
Thread: machine embroidery threads of
   colors matching the covering fabric
Tracing paper as needed
Stabilizer as need

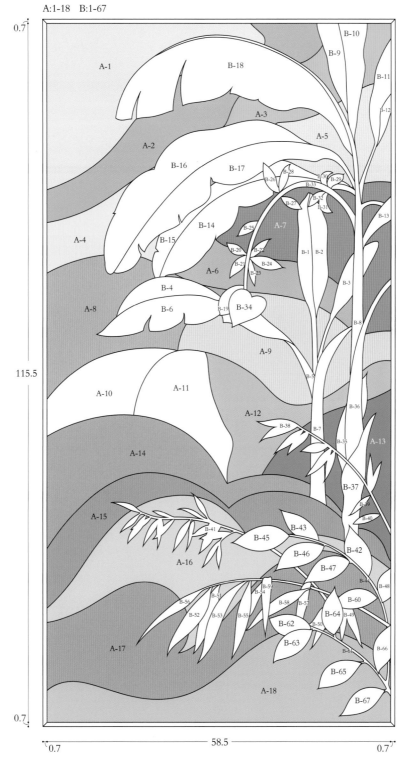

A:1-18 B:1-67

0.7

115.5

0.7

0.7 58.5 0.7

Template

Thin Blanket

Supplies

Completed size: 155.5 × 155.5 cm
Fabric scraps: various colors and sizes
Backing fabric: 175.5 × 175.5 cm

General-purpose batting:
  165.5 × 165.5 cm
Grid paper as needed

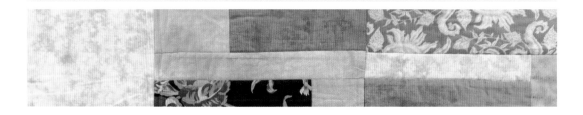

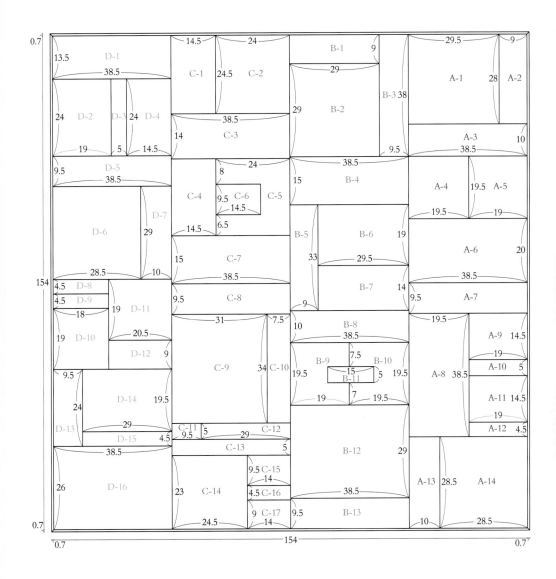

Template

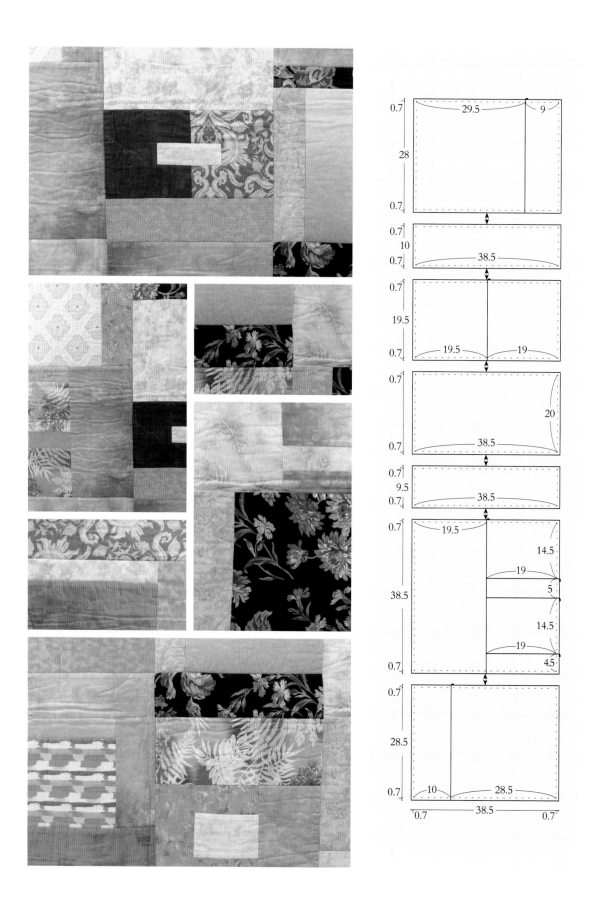

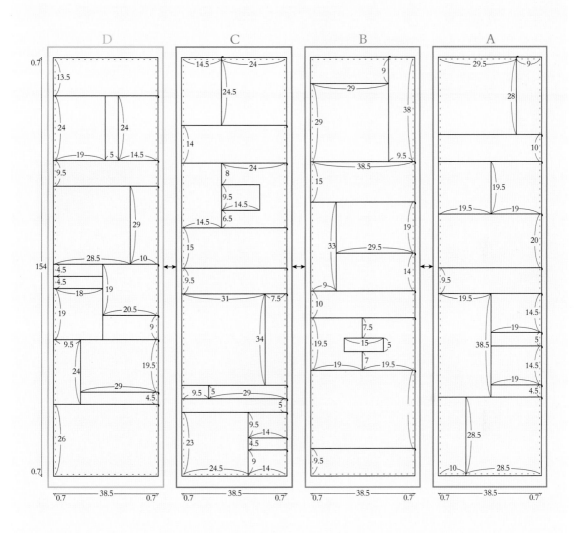

1 Cut the fabrics to the sizes shown in the illustration, using the technique of Machine Sewing: Blocks of Different sizes (page 45), and number them. Piece the patches one by one in the order shown in the illustration to finish the covering fabric. The blanket consists of four larger patches (see above), and the pieces for each patch should be joined together first (see the illustration on facing page).

2 Lay the backing, the batting, and the covering on top of each other and pin them up. Sew them together using stitching in the ditch (page 54). You may prefer freestyle stitching.

3 Trim the edges of the stitched work, using a seam allowance of 0.8 cm. Make bias tapes using a 3.5 cm strip and finish all the raw edges.

Cushion with Leaf Pattern

Supplies

Completed size: 45 × 45 cm
Background fabric: 50 × 50 cm
Fabric scraps: various colors and sizes
Backing fabric: 50 × 70 cm
One-sided adhesive batting:
   50 × 50 cm
Grid paper: 50 × 50 cm

1 Make a copy of the template as it is.

2 Choose fabrics in colors you like for the background, the decorative patches, and the backing. The background and the decorative patches are for the front of the cushion, and the backing fabric is for the back.

3 Iron the background fabric well. Draw a square of 45 × 45 cm on it, and cut it out, using a seam allowance of 1 cm.

4 Transfer the desgin onto the background fabric using a copyboard or carbon paper. The tracing lines should be erasable or thin enough to be covered for a better finish.

5 Delineate the seven leaves on the grid paper and number them. Cut each of them out as paper patterns.

6 Pick your fabric and iron it flat. Transfer the pattern onto the wrong side of the fabric.

7 Cut each of the patterns out, using a seam allowance of 3 mm.

8 Lay the leaves in the corresponding places on the background fabric and pin them up. Hold them in place using basting stitches with a seam allowance of at least 3 mm.

9 Fold inward about 3 mm from the edges of the leaves. Match each of them with their outlines on the background fabric. Sew along the outline of leaves, using appliqué stitch (page 62). For a better finish, fold the edge when you are 2–3 cm away from it.

10 Once the seven leaves are stitched onto the background fabric, the covering of the cushion is done. Cut the batting to 45 × 45 cm. With the adhesive side of the batting and the wrong side of the covering together, pin them up. Run a warm iron over the right side of the covering so that the two are held together.

11 Sew around the edges of the leaves using stitches in the ditch. Where there is enough blank space, you may want to be more creative and use freestyle stitching.

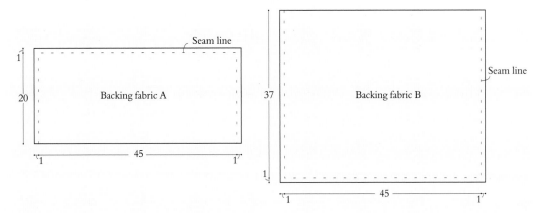

12 Draw the seam line shown in the illustration and cut it out.

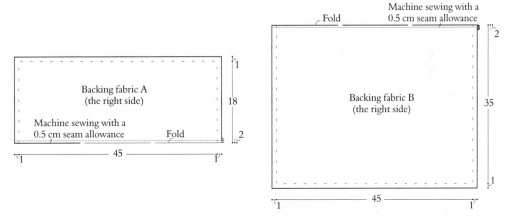

13 Fold inward about 1 cm on the longer edges of backing fabric A and B. Repeat for another 1 cm of the edge. Machine stitch a straight line along the edge, using a 0.5–0.7 cm seam allowance.

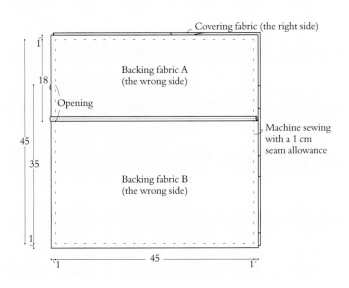

14 With the right sides together, stitch the four sides along the seam lines. Turn the right side out through the opening (the overlapping parts of A and B). Iron the four edges well. Tuck a pillow inner inside, and you're finished!

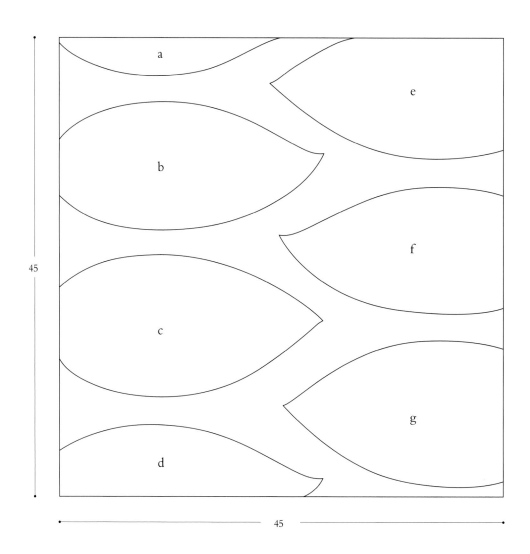

45

45

a

b

c

d

e

f

g

Template

Cushion with an X Pattern

Supplies

Completed size: 45 × 45 cm

Fabric scraps: various colors and sizes

Backing fabric: 50 × 70 cm

One-sided adhesive batting: 50 × 50 cm

Grid paper: 50 × 50 cm

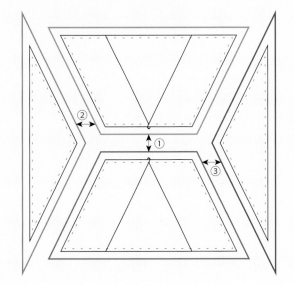

1 Draw the patterns on the grid paper and number them.

2 Cut out the patterns A, B, and C.

3 Following the Machine Sewing: Blocks of Different Sizes (page 45), draw seam lines on the wrong side of the fabric and cut them out.

4 In the order indicated, machine stitch the covering fabric and iron it flat.

5 Finish the project following steps 12–14 for Cushion with Leaf Pattern.

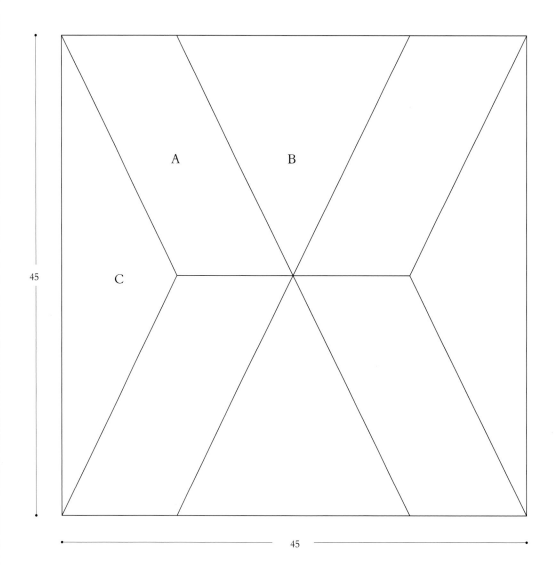

45

45

A

B

C

Template

Tablecloth

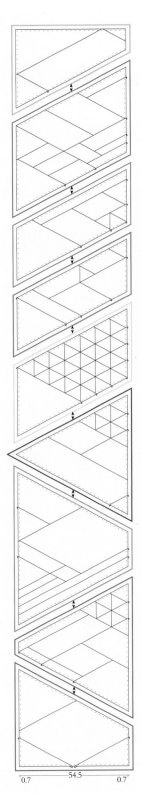

Supplies

Completed size: 279.5 × 137 cm
Fabric scraps: various colors and sizes
Backing fabric: 310 × 170 cm
Double-sided adhesive interlining: 295 × 150 cm

1 Make a copy of the template as it is. Cut all the patches out.

2 Cut the fabric for all the patches. Place a paper patch on the wrong side of the fabric, mark the ends, join the ends with a rule, and draw the seam lines. Number them with a pencil on the wrong side of the fabric.

3 Cut the patches out using a seam allowance of 7 mm. Arrange them with reference to the composition.

0.7   54.5   0.7

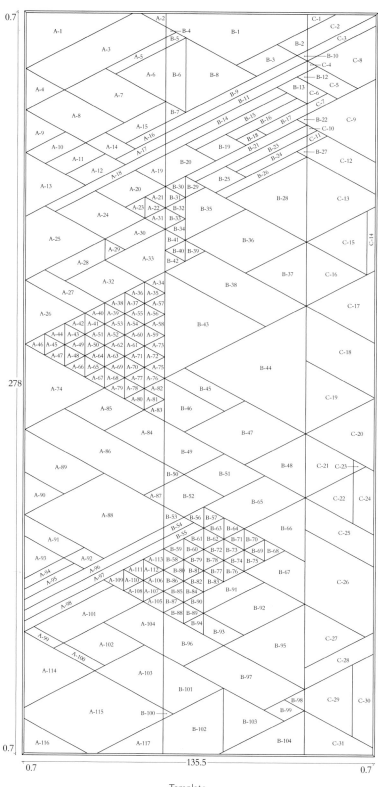

Template

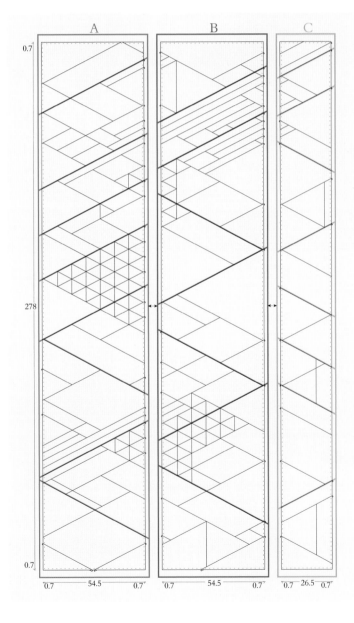

A B C

0.7

278

0.7

0.7 54.5 0.7" 0.7 54.5 0.7" 0.7 26.5 0.7"

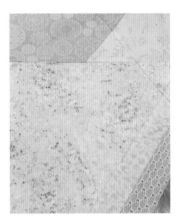

4 Join the patches in the order shown in the illustration and iron them well. The illustration on page shows how the larger patches in section A are divided and joined together (on page 121). The colored lines in the illustration on the left will help you to recognize larger patches.

5 Cut the backing fabric 8 cm larger than the covering all round. Iron it flat.

6 Cut the double-sided interlining 5 cm larger than the covering all round. With the wrong side of the backing fabric facing you, lay the interlining right in the middle of it (the interlining not only allows for a better finish, but helps the two layers of fabric to stick better). With its right side facing you, place the covering fabric in the middle over the interlining. Run a warm iron over the layers to hold them together.

7 Trim the edges of the three layers using a seam allowance of 0.8 cm. Make bias tapes using a 3.5 cm strip and finish all the raw edges.

2. The *Shanglin Garden* Series

This project drew its inspiration from *Ode to Shanglin Garden* written by Sima Xiangru for the Daoist garden that was built for Qin Shi Huang, the first emperor of a unified China. As I have mentioned in Chapter 2, no one knows where the garden was, but the poem describes how the best part of the emperor's land, where there were mountains, forests, rivers, waterfalls, and lakes, was used as the first royal garden in China.

As my conception of the royal garden, this project attempts to combine the painting styles of Ming dynasty artists Ni Zan (1301–1374) and Qiu Ying (c. 1498–1552) and traditional Chinese gardening elements such as rockwork, pools, trees, and flowers. Modern perspectives and techniques are used to adapt it to an in-house setting.

Templates for part of the wall hanging, cushions, tablecloth, and rugs are introduced below, and their techniques are explained for readers who might be interested in creating their own designs.

Wall Hanging

Supplies

Completed size: 111.5 × 101.5 cm
White background fabric: 120 × 110 cm
Fabric scraps: various colors and sizes
General-purpose batting: 130 × 120cm
Backing fabric: 140 × 130 cm
Thread: machine embroidery threads of colors matching covering fabric
Tracing paper: 120 × 110 cm
Stabilizer as needed

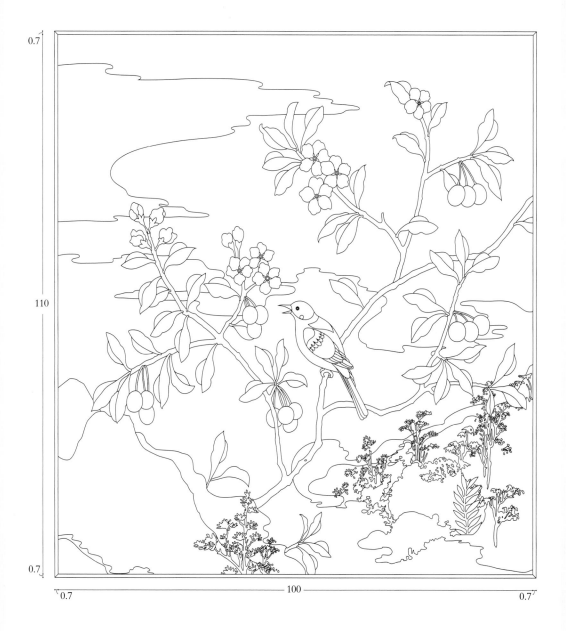

0.7

110

0.7

0.7 ⊢——— 100 ———⊣ 0.7

Template

1　This project shares much of the work for the wall hangings in the *Three and All* series. Make a copy of the template as it is. You can number the patches according to the layers of the patterns. Complete the covering following steps 1–6 for the wall hangings in the *Three and All* series.

2　Remove the covering from the foam and tear off the tracing paper. As the design is more complicated, appliqué stitch is recommended for the parts with the most intricate details, while appliquéing by machine can be used for the other parts. Handle the covering fabric with care to stop the surface from piling.

3　With reference to step 8 for the wall hanging in the *Three and All* series, pin up the backing, the batting, and the covering and sew along the edges using stitching in the ditch. Where there is enough blank space, you might prefer a freestyle stitching technique. However, too many stitches may spoil your project.

4　Following steps 9–10 for the wall hangings in the *Three and All* series, complete the work for the frame and then finish the raw edges.

Cushions

Supplies

Completed size: 45 × 45 cm
Background fabric: 50 × 50 cm
Fabric scraps: various colors and sizes

Backing fabric: 50 × 70 cm
One-sided adhesive batting: 50 × 50 cm
Grid paper: 50 × 50 cm

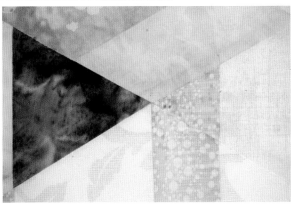

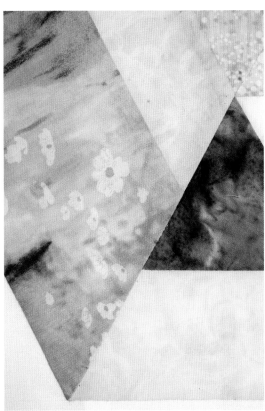

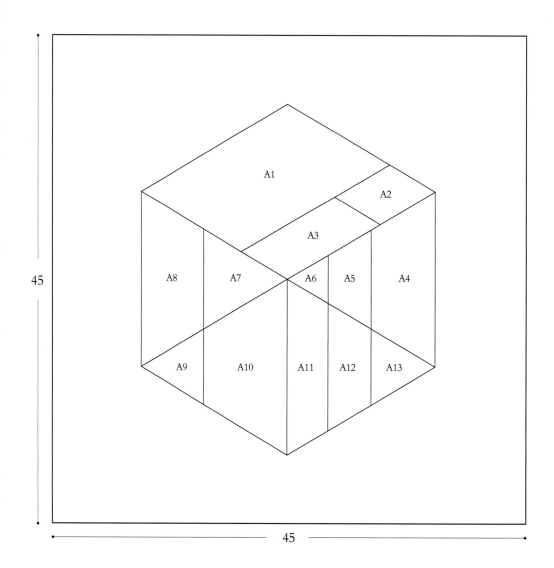

45

45

Template for Cushion A

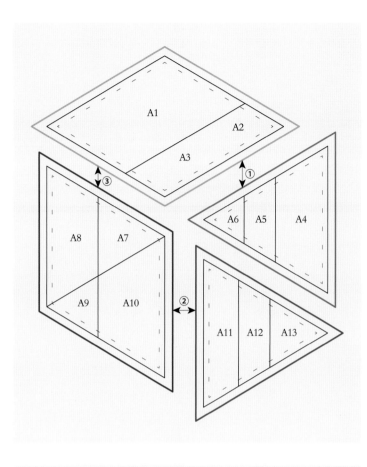

1 While the techniques for Cushion A are explained, only the templates for the other three designs are included. The first step is to print the template for Cushion A onto paper.

2 Choose the background fabric, fabric scraps, and backing fabric, with reference to steps 2–4 for the Cushion with Leaf Pattern in the *Three and All* series. Iron the background fabric well, and cut it out. Copy the outline of the design onto the background.

3 Make paper patterns following the template. Draw seam lines onto the fabric and cut it out, leaving an allowance of 0.7 cm all round.

4 Stitch the pieces together in the order indicated, and iron it well. Make sure that you stop before the circled points in the illustration (see the two illustiations on the left).

5 With the help of a rule, use a bone folder to mark the wrong side of the covering fabric along the outer seam line. Press the allowance inside and iron it well, so that you have a clear edge.

6 Place it on top of the background fabric, aligning the outline seams. Hold them in place with pins, and bast with loose stitches.

7 Remove the pins. Hand sew the patches by using appliqué stitch (page 62), so that the stitches do not show. You may prefer machine sewing instead.

8 Once all the patches are done, cut out the batting to 45 × 45 cm. With the adhesive side of the batting facing the wrong side of the background fabric, hold them in place with pins and run a warm iron over the right side of the background fabric.

9 Go over steps 12–14 for the Cushion with Leaf Pattern in the *Three and All* series for the other side of the cushion, and you're finished.

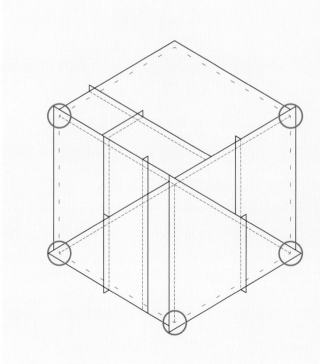

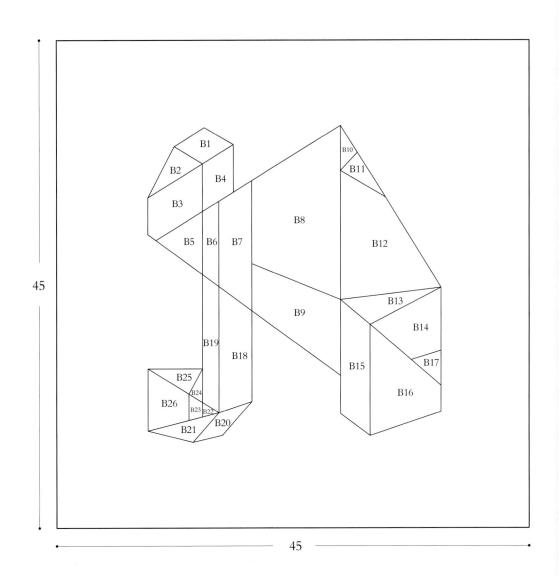

45

45

Template for Cushion B

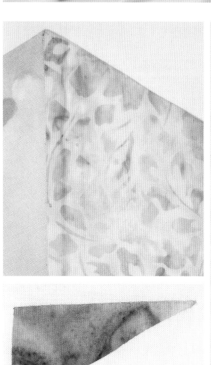

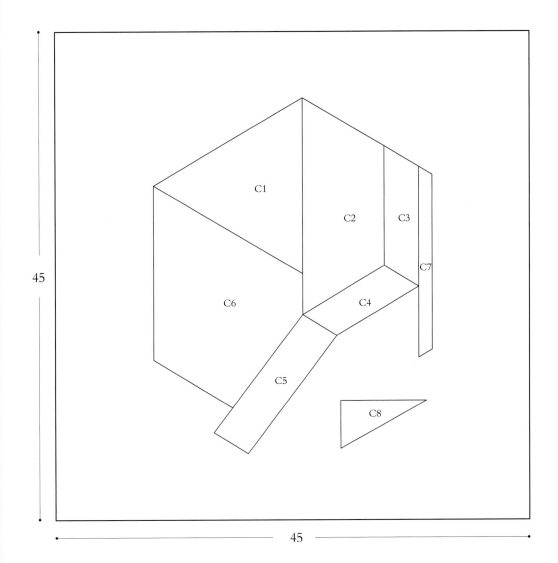

45

45

Template for Cushion C

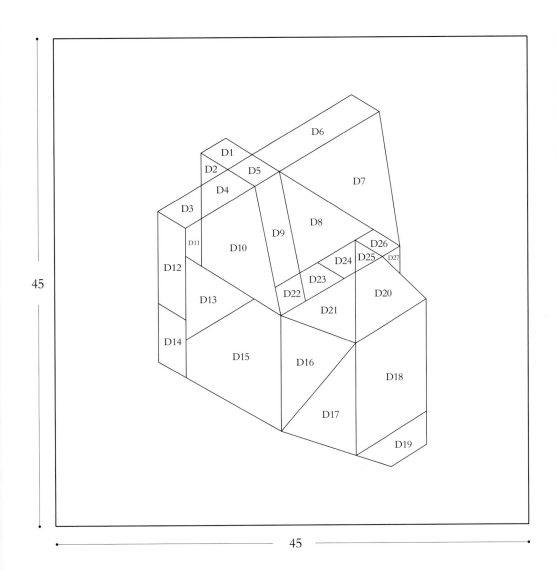

45

45

Template for Cushion D

Tablecloth

Supplies

Completed size: 279.5 × 137 cm
Fabric scraps: various colors and
   sizes

Backing fabric: 310 × 170 cm
Double-sided adhesive interlining:
   295 × 150 cm

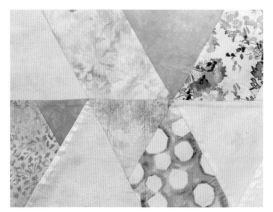

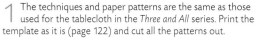

1 The techniques and paper patterns are the same as those used for the tablecloth in the *Three and All* series. Print the template as it is (page 122) and cut all the patterns out.

2 Cut the scraps according to their colors, leaving enough of a seam allowance. Arrange them according to your composition.

3 Stitch them together, then iron them well.

4 Cut the backing fabric out and iron it flat.

5 Cut the interlining to the proper size. Place the backing fabric, the interlining, and the covering fabric on top of each other, and iron them together.

6 Trim the layers with a rotary cutter along a line about 0.8 cm away from the contours. Make your bias tapes, and finish all of the raw edges.

Carpet

Supplies

Completed size: 150 × 150 cm
Fabric scraps: various colors and sizes
Backing fabric: 170 × 170 cm

Batting for machine sewing: 160 × 160 cm
Tracing paper: 160 × 160 cm
Tear-away stablizer: 300 × 110 cm

1 Appliquéing by machine (page 48) is used for the covering fabric, following the covering techniques for the wall hanging of this series. Fabric should be chosen in reference to the patterns, and stabilizer is used.

2 Lay the backing, the batting, and the covering on top of each other and pin them up. Sew them together using stitching in the ditch and freestyle stitches. You can choose decorative patterns if you like.

3 Make your bias tapes, and finish all the raw edges.

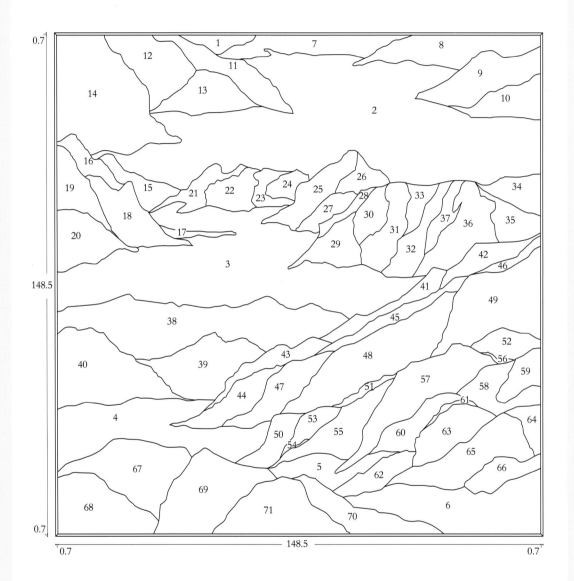

Template